RHYTHMS
of a Himalayan Village

R H Y

OF A HIMA

T H M S
L A Y A N   V I L L A G E

H U G H   R .   D O W N S

HARPER & ROW, PUBLISHERS
San Francisco

Cambridge
Hagerstown
Philadelphia
New York

1817

London
Mexico City
São Paulo
Sydney

Photos on pages 20 and 23 are courtesy of Ngawong Lekshi, upper Parakshey, Nepal. He told me that the latter was taken by "the English"; I think it may have been taken by the Rutledge expedition of 1933.

Photo on page 24 appears in *A Photographic Record of the Mount Jolmo Lungma Scientific Expedition*, Science Press, Peking, 1974.

Selections from *The Vimalakīrti Nirdeśa Sūtra*, translated by Charles Luk [Lu K'uan Yü], pp. 86, 90, copyright © 1972 by Charles Luk, and from *The Tibetan Book of the Dead*, translated by Francesca Fremantle and Chögyam Trungpa, pp. 98-99, copyright © 1975 by Francesca Fremantle and Chögyam Trungpa, are reprinted by special arrangement with Shambhala Publications, Inc., 1123 Spruce Street, Boulder, Colorado 80302.

Selections from *The Royal Song of Saraha: A Study in the History of Buddhist Thought*, by Herbert V. Guenther, pp. 65, 66, 67, copyright © 1968 by the University of Washington Press, are reprinted by special arrangement with the University of Washington Press.

Selection from *Buddhist Texts Through the Ages*, edited and translated by Edward Conze, I. B. Horner, D. Snellgrove, and A. Waley, p. 296, copyright © 1954, is reprinted by special arrangement with Bruno Cassirer (Publishers) Ltd.

FIRST EDITION
Designed by Paul Quin

Library of Congress Cataloging in Publication Data
Downs, Hugh R.
  Rhythms of a Himalayan village.

  Bibliography: p 225.
  1. Sherpas.   2. Nepal—Description and travel.
I. Title.
DS493.9.S5D68   1980   954.9'6   79-2983
ISBN 0-06-250240-9

80 81 82 83 84 10 9 8 7 6 5 4 3 2 1

CONTENTS

ACKNOWLEDGMENTS

I am greatly indebted to many people for their help in the preparation of this volume. Foremost is Ngawong Lekshi, or Au Leshi, without whose exemplary way of life and overwhelming kindness I might never have had the inspiration. Dr. Thomas D. Nicholson of the American Museum of Natural History, Noel Cobb, Anny Chen, Robert and Margaret Klein, and my parents, Ruth and Hugh Downs, all helped mold this project at various stages of its incompletion. Michael Katz was especially helpful in initiating me into the ritual of publication.

Special thanks also to Dr. Barbara Aziz, Tony Guida, Matthew Kapstein, and the Rev. Dr. Kurt Schwalbe, all of whom have lived for extended periods of time among the people depicted in this book. They have corrected errors and added information, and I am very grateful to them. Tony and I spent many months together with Au Leshi; Tony's humor and inquisitive spirit often sparked conversations of tremendous interest. Matthew contributed translations of two poems composed by Tulshig Rimpoche and generously lent his meticulous erudition to help guide these pages to greater accuracy.

I would also like to thank His Majesty's Government of Nepal—both the offices of Immigration and of the Inspector General of Police—for their cooperation and assistance during my four-year residence in Nepal.

Mimi Church, my constant companion, has been the most help. She has contributed unselfishly far beyond what would be expected, acting as first mate, critic, and compassionate Bodhisattva. I am tremendously thankful to a wonderful woman.

INTRODUCTION

For about two years I lived near a small Sherpa village in northeastern Nepal. That brief stay occupies a position of rare prominence in my memory, and the friendships cultivated during that time still bear incomparable fruit.

I have always been restless, unsatisfied with what my surroundings provided. When I became an adult, the prospect of material gain — elegant food and clothing — wasn't attractive. I could see people who had all those things, and I was unconvinced that they were satisfied — from time to time satiated perhaps, but never satisfied. Observing that people who, according to the criteria of society, should have been content were not, I arrived at that curious juncture of appearance and substance, where things are not as they appear.

Fascinated by that discrepancy, I stumbled into the related world of symbol and its use in iconographic representations. I did not stumble for long; indeed, I very quickly fell flat on my face. The worlds of symbol and iconographic art necessitate guidance. What do all those symbols mean, anyway?

India offers not only a wide selection of iconographic material but 400 million opinions to assist in interpreting it. After only a few months in India, however, and having surveyed only a fraction of the population, I moved on to the neighboring mountain kingdom of Nepal. I continued asking questions like, Why is that deity sitting on a lion? What's he doing with the sword? After living in Nepal for two years, I was sufficiently fluent in the Nepali language to embark on more formal training with a Sherpa painter. I stayed in Nepal another two years, studying with the Sherpas.

I studied for a few months with one painter, a layman; then I discovered a monk named Au Leshi who painted. He gently guided my poor attempts to paw out the drawing of a deity according to canonical proportions, correcting a measurement here or the grace of a curve there.

More important, however, than any of the artistic skills he imparted was his behavior, which engendered a sense of why his way of life is called traditional. The Latin root of tradition, *tradere*, means to hand over: one of the most valuable characteristics of our species is the ability to pass on our experiences. The knowledge that is handed over in traditional societies is of two sorts. People learn how to make fires, to farm, and to build houses; in addition, they learn something of themselves. Sherpas explicitly recognize this bifurcation of knowledge by referring to outer and inner wealth. Those who have attained inner wealth are rare, even among the Sherpas. When noticed, however, they are accorded decidedly more esteem than those who have acquired outer wealth.

To hand over knowledge of the outer world, we often give someone a tool and demonstrate its use. The recipient can then practice and master the new skill. Passing on knowledge of the inner world is more difficult. There is nothing substantive, such as a plow or an adze, that can be handed over. The tools can only be represented symbolically; the student must discover the tool, and its proper use, himself. Representations of one thing by another are like little ligaments that transmute all the myriad things into a single universe. Without a sense of symbol these ligaments remain unnoticed, and much of our experience appears unsatisfactory—disjointed, separate, or scattered.

Undisturbed by this tendency toward fragmentation, Au Leshi seemed content. He never asked for anything; whatever people gave him was what he wanted. His apparent satisfaction did nothing to ameliorate my discontent. Whenever I was restless he responded by saying, "Ask yourself, Where is the desire coming from? What color is it? What shape is it?" I had always believed that one could find something—if not a possession, then a philosophy—that would satisfy one's desire. Au Leshi's constant admonitions slowly chipped away at this conviction.

I once lamented that my inability to read and speak Tibetan fluently might thwart his teaching. He broke out laughing and said, "What you're after, you're not going to find in any language."

Nothing happened during this stay with him. I learned painting techniques, cooking skills, garden craft, and things like that. But I never found anything that I could point to and say, "This is it."

I left Nepal and went on to live in Taiwan, Japan, and California. Occasionally I remember Au Leshi's uproarious laughter as he looked at me saying, "Well, did you find it?" I never found it. In fact the constant repetition of his comic jibing left me with the distinct impression that if I ever did find anything—even a thought, an idea, or a feeling—I should beware, because it would belong to the outside world.

However emphatically Au Leshi disparaged the pursuit of palliatives for restlessness, he respected and encouraged attempts to look for the source of discontent. There certainly is nothing to be found in this book that could satisfy anyone who seeks an answer. But it does reflect several ways of looking that were presented to me as important by a number of Sherpas.

The photographs in this book were taken partly as gifts for the people depicted, and partly because I have always taken photographs. Over the years, when friends have asked what in the world I did for all that time in the Himalayas, I've pulled out my photographs and started telling stories, and each time the stories have changed the initial appearance of the photographs. This alteration reflected my own experience, and my friends entered that world of evaporating appearances where Au Leshi roams so comfortably.

As I described two particular events—an annual Sherpa dance festival called Maṇi Rimdu and a Sherpa funeral—I noticed a close affinity between them: both are dramas. The dance festival is a public performance, with only a few participants playing formal roles. Though the funeral is a private affair, it has a universal intimacy; all of us will have a part to play in at least one death.

Maṇi Rimdu tells a story in dance. Ostensibly the dancers reenact the establishment of Buddhism in Tibet. Yet hidden within this drama of cultural history, say many Sherpas, is the story of an individual's awakening.

The funeral is also a drama; the staging is prescribed by ritual texts, as are the words and actions of the participants. And, as in the festival, there is a strong sense of things being otherwise than they appear. Although the sobering fact of death was everywhere evident at my friend's funeral, those involved assumed that what seemed like an end was a beginning. They spoke to the deceased, made an appointment with him for a year later, and offered him food. They even described what he was seeing at the moment and urged him not to be afraid.

Learning about the interpretations of the festival, and being invited to the funeral as an extended family member, grew out of friendships with several craftsmen. Primarily image makers, they daily investigate the relationship between the image and what it imitates. This investigation does not produce mere clever interpretations of symbols, but generates an examination of the tension between appearance and perception. This analysis naturally extends to every activity in life.

I have arranged this book in three sections. The first, "Celebration," introduces the Sherpa world in general, then concentrates on the Maṇi Rimdu festival with its dance play.

The second section, "Vocation," focuses on a few craftsmen. The skills they develop by examining illusion can dispel one reality and allow us to move on to another. We, as observers of craft, can become totally absorbed by a compelling performance, or by the charm of a convincing painting. These artists not only practice awakening from the fascination their art creates; they also try to awaken from those everyday beguilements the world has in store for everyone.

The third section, "Return," records a Sherpa funeral service and the cremation of a man's expended bodily vehicle. Throughout, the participants try to see through the illusory identification with the body. No one is fooled by the cessation of bodily processes; everyone agrees that it indicates a beginning. The man is reduced to his store of inner wealth—an inner equity that is no longer bound to the tangible plane.

In the quiet of the forest, the infinitely fading moments of the present become a day, day, night. These lights and darks become weeks. Ever so slowly, these weeks gather into seasons and become hot, become rainy, become cold, and become hot again. The winters are neither better nor worse than the monsoons; they are simply different parts of a cycle. When things change, we feel deprived, but we are always free to step back and see all change as part of a larger composition. The notion that one's life will be improved by holding on to possessions, people, or ideas becomes absurd when one encounters the ineluctable rhythms of change.

Hugh R. Downs

Pachim Gufa
Buddha Jayanti 1979

CELEBRATION

When (in winter) still water by the wind is stirred,
It takes (as ice) the shape and texture of a rock.
When the deluded are disturbed by interpretive thoughts,
That which is as yet unpatterned turns very hard and solid.

Saraha
Dohākoṣa

      In a valley of northeastern Nepal sits the Sherpa village called Gompa Zhung, from the quiet sting of winter to the flush of summer. About a six-day walk to Tibet and a two-week walk to India, Gompa Zhung is five days from the nearest motorable road.

This was one of the earliest villages to be settled by the Sherpa ancestors, perhaps as early as the fifteenth century. The word *Sherpa* comes from two Tibetan words—*shar* meaning east, and *pa* meaning people. There is a strong belief among the Sherpas that they migrated to Nepal from Kham, a province in eastern Tibet that borders on Szechwan province in China. The reasons for this migration are unclear today, but it may have been provoked by Mongol plundering.

Most foreigners are familiar with the Sherpas only through their fame as load bearers and guides for mountaineering expeditions, yet such work is a recent and superficial aspect of their culture. When we put aside our glimpse of Sherpas as servants, we can penetrate to more subtle levels of their experience.

Gompa Zhung, like most Sherpa villages, sits amid small farming plots bounded by squat stone walls. Farming is not easy here, but it is done. In the valleys between the steep mountains, potatoes and wheat are cultivated. There are also small gardens of turnips, chives, and onions. Corn does manage to grow in Gompa Zhung, though it doesn't flourish in higher villages. Everyone—men, women, and children—shares the responsibilities for a successful harvest. The farmer can be heard yelling at the draft animal, a cow-yak cross called a *zopkio*. The fields are rocky; hail comes often to these parts when it's cold. The monsoon turns fields, yards, and trails to mud during the summer, and with the water the famous Himalayan leeches come out, hanging fat on both cattle and humans. Despite these difficulties, the farmers have food at harvest. Producing food is the basic activity of all Sherpas; every Sherpa, even one involved in business, has at least a small plot to work, and this supplement feeds the family even when they have no money.

Farming feeds other hungers besides that of the stomach. The earth falls under the special protection of a deity called *Sai-nying-po*, and the farmer assists this force quite consciously and quite proudly. Sherpas like to tell about the exploits of their heroes, who are sometimes farmers. Great spiritual quests, which elicit the highest regard among these people, may occur in the midst of mundane activities like plowing a field. Because myth and daily life are interwoven, farming provides both food and meaning.

Upon the bad field of desires,
I spread the fertilizer of the Preparatory Practice;
. . .
I plant the seeds of the Nonconfusing Mind,
Farming with discriminative thought.
. . .
With these tools and efforts, the bud of Bodhi sprouts;
In due season ripe will be my fruit.

Milarepa
The Hundred Thousand Songs of Milarepa

They build solid comfortable homes, generally of stone, with wooden trim and plank floors. Glass can be found in a weekly bazaar a four-hour walk from the village. Window glass at the bazaar has already been carried five days from the road that connects with Kathmandu, the capital of Nepal. Since this glass is expensive, most windows are covered with a locally made paper. The houses are usually two stories high. The lower story is used for storage and for housing animals, the upper for cooking and living.

Because of the proximity of the dwellings, everyone knows everyone else; brother and sister are common terms of address among adults who may not be related by blood but who feel they share in each other's lives. Being a neighbor is a serious occupation and adds to the security of the village. It is inconceivable to remain anonymous within these friendly precincts.

The lower valleys of the Sherpas, in an area called Solu, have denser forests than the higher valleys, called Khumbu. Solu Sherpas take great pride in their carpentry skills. Not only the homes, but the articles in them, nearly all wooden, are often handsomely crafted. Tables, bowls, butter crocks, flagons—everything is solidly built and, as is so characteristic of wooden articles, improves with age. Common Sherpa household articles are often fondled and caressed by foreign visitors whose native lands suffer from a paucity of handcrafted implements.

The fabrication of wooden products is much more a testimony to the craftsman's skill than to the sophistication of his tools. The adze has not been a standard implement of carpenters in the West for a good many years. In Solu, however, it is the mainstay of the craft. The refinement of this particular skill can only seem uncanny to those of us who are uninitiated.

The carpenter . . . explains what "mystery" there is in his art: "I first reduce my mind to absolute quiescence. . . . I enter some mountain forest, I search for a suitable tree. It contains the form required, which is afterwards elaborated. I see the thing in my mind's eye, and then set to work." . . . It is not the accident of genius, but a pure humanity that is essential.

Ananda K. Coomaraswamy
"Chinese Painting at Boston"

Sherpas put wooden shingles, weighted down by stones, on the roof. A high wind, which is not uncommon, may leave a few shingles out of line, thus creating a leak in the roof. Nobody ever seems to mind; it's a small job to jump up and correct the position of an errant shingle.

Most houses have at least one prayer flag out in front — long strips of cotton printed with woodblock impressions of a horse, deities, and a prayer or two. Sherpas call the flag *lung ta*, or wind horse, as they believe that a being of this description transports the edifying message printed on the flag. They believe the mind to be a sense, like sight and hearing. The message of the flag can be assimilated through any sensory receptor. Feeling the wind in one's face or hearing the flutter of cloth both provide access to the message, just as reading and understanding do. The variety of sensible beings who profit from prayer flags includes birds of the air and leeches in the mud, as well as human beings.

The prayer flags are one of the many devices used by the Sherpas to practice giving without expectation of reward. It is not cheap to erect such flags; long, straight trees must be cut and dragged to the spot. After the flags are up, they don't make the crops grow better, provide shelter, or keep one free from disease. But in constructing such ostensibly useless things, the builder unselfishly edifies others without anticipating personal gain.

The hearth, on the second floor, is the center of the house, not geometrically, but for domestic affairs. The fire sees a constant preparation of tea. A rich brew churned with butter, milk, and salt, Sherpa tea is really more of a soup, and quite welcome in the rain or cold. Meals are prepared on an average of twice a day. There are two basic menus: boiled potatoes, or a thick flour paste called *sen*, which is made from toasted barley or wheat flour added to boiling water. A lump of *sen* is broken off and molded about one's thumb. Jokingly referred to as a Sherpa spoon, it is used to scoop up an accompanying vegetable broth.

The fire is not only a social focus, but it is respected as a deity. Hindus, who live to the south of the Sherpas, identify this element with the ancient Vedic god of fire, Agni. The Sherpas, who are Buddhists, inherited their respect for fire from the older tradition, although they are probably not aware of this historical connection between Hinduism and Buddhism. These remnants of what some might be quick to label primitive nature worship in practice provide a sensible code for maintaining one's surroundings. It would be gauche to spit into a fire, and odiferous refuse is meticulously kept away from a fire out of respect. Even in the lower valleys, where there is more wood than at higher elevations, the fire cannot be used as a heat source except as a peripheral benefit. Sherpas use their wood conservatively; when a specific task is completed, they pull out the logs and snuff them in the ash. As a decoration, or a gift, occasionally a juniper sprig is thrown onto a fire just for its delightful smell.

Life here, like anywhere else, is not without its pleasures. *Chang*, a sweet-tasting, thick, and potent beer, is frequently brewed from wheat or barley, sometimes maize or millet, or even rice, which must be imported on someone's back from lower regions. A distillation, known as *arak*, is also made. These are both home brews par excellence. Their quality varies tremendously from household to household, and the skill that a family demonstrates in the manufacture of spirits can determine its social prestige to a certain degree. These beverages are often proferred to guests in a remarkable rapid sequence of three compulsory cupfuls, to the excited shouts of *"Shay, shay,"* or "Drink, drink."

Although the way Sherpas live and the things they eat may seem strange to an outsider, the children and the aged provide familiar images to any living person. When Sherpas grow old, they retire from customary duties. For them, old age provides time for introspection, time to take stock of one's achievements and to prepare oneself for coming transitions—above all, a time for great pride in being old. As one ages, the opportunity arises to see through the illusions that life presents and to penetrate to what is constant amid change. This woman in her seventies grinds zinc oxide, a white paint. Grinding the pigment that will be used to paint a deity is considered a meritorious act.

The Sherpa aged are often involved with monastery life, although they do not necessarily become monks or nuns. In fact, monasteries are the core of Sherpa cultural activity; they maintain the literature and hence the traditional education of the young as well as of the old.

*For what rational being would stand or sit or lie at ease, still less
laugh, when he knows of old age, disease, and death?
But he is just like a being without reason, who, on seeing another
aged or ill or even dead, remains indifferent and unmoved.*

Aśvaghoṣa
Buddhacarita: Acts of the Buddha

The Sherpas follow the Tibetan Buddhist tradition. Originally imported to Tibet from India between the seventh and eleventh centuries, and modified by Tibetan culture, this expression of Buddhism has had an especially strong influence in Nepal, Mongolia, and parts of China. For at least the past four centuries, there has been a small migration of Tibetans into areas occupied by Sherpas. In the 1950s, after China occupied Tibet, many Tibetans came to Nepal, where the constitution guarantees religious freedom. The Nepalese very generously extended their hospitality to the many Tibetans who felt themselves unable to pursue their Buddhist activities in their homeland.

One such man, a *lama* (or teacher) called Tulshig Rimpoche, has settled in the main Solu valley of Nepal. All forms of Buddhism emphasize the importance of a teacher, someone who literally embodies the teaching of the Buddha and vitalizes the written word. Any monk may be called a lama, as indeed any layman who assumes certain religious responsibilities may. The title *Rimpoche*, which means precious one, is reserved for widely respected lamas. In Tibetan *tul* means illusion; *shig* means kill; hence, this teacher's name means precious destroyer of illusion.

Ignorant are they who do not recognize the evanescence of worldly things and who tenaciously cleave to them as final realities; . . . ignorant are those who do not understand that there is no such thing as an ego-soul. . . . Buddhism, therefore, most emphatically maintains that . . . we must radically dispel this illusion, this ignorance, this root of all evil and suffering in this life.

D. T. Suzuki
Outlines of Mahayana Buddhism

Tulshig Rimpoche is a reincarnate lama, or *tulku*, in Tibetan. As a small child of two or three years, he spoke about his previous life. A lama whom he had taught in his former incarnation found him as a boy and recognized the Tulshig Rimpoche. He received his education as a monk; he is recognized as a meditator. This photograph of him was taken in Kathmandu in the late 1950s, when he was about thirty.

Although Tulshig Rimpoche sits ensconced in gold brocades and luxurious trappings, he does not seek wealth. The Buddhist goal of equanimity stresses the danger of clinging. It makes no difference if one clings to material possessions or to asceticism. One must be aware of the grasping; the outward form the attachment assumes is immaterial.

Many have given gifts of gold, silk, wool, and livestock to Tulshig Rimpoche to encourage his work. The bulk of these remain in Tibet. When he left his monastery and traveled to Nepal, he wrote a poem describing the frivolity of believing in outward forms of wealth and the transitoriness of all life's manifestations.

An uninvited guest has arrived:
    rising over the peak to the East,
    the auspicious moon is like the medicinal jasmine,
    soothing the sore afflictions of Tibet.
    This is the occasion for a festive and honeyed shower of joy.

When you tame the enemy within your own mind—
    I, myself, subject and object —
the demonic armies of the ten directions
will just fall in defeat by themselves.
What need then have I of gurus and lords,
    who are hardened by hope and fear?

The retinue formed by the spontaneous presence
of one's own awareness is naturally complete.
What need then have I of a native land,
    filled with the deceptions of passion and hatred?

Arriving now in the wilderness,
    in an uncertain place of solitude,
accompanied by unbiased spiritual friends,
I have drawn forth this song of separation
    for the fulfillment of myself and all others.

        Composed by Tulshig Dharmamati [Tulshig Rimpoche]

Ngawong Tenzin Norbu founded Tulshig Rimpoche's monastery at Dzarongpu, in Tibet near the Nepal border. Sherpa pilgrimages to Dzarongpu, as well as Ngawong Tenzin Norbu's visits to Nepal, encouraged the establishment of many major Sherpa monasteries. Even before his move to Nepal, Tulshig Rimpoche, like his teacher Ngawong Tenzin Norbu, had many followers among the Sherpas.

Tulshig Rimpoche's followers believe that he, like many other lamas, reassumes a human body after death in order to return and aid his disciples. The previous incarnation of Tulshig Rimpoche spent several years at Dzarongpu monastery and served as one of Ngawong Tenzin Norbu's teachers. He promised to return in his next life, so at Tulshig's death Ngawong Tenzin Norbu sought and found his reincarnation. The current Tulshig Rimpoche then came to the monastery and studied with Ngawong Tenzin Norbu. This relationship between teacher and student, in which a teacher returns to study from his former student, maintains the lineage over generations.

Every lama embodies the doctrine in his own style. It was widely agreed that Ngawong Tenzin Norbu was most like the historical Buddha in the way he taught and in his manner of understanding. There are stories of very small children who would point and impulsively call him *Sangye*, the Tibetan word for Buddha. He became known as Dzarongpu Sangye — the Buddha of Dzarongpu.

Tulshig Rimpoche's monastery in Tibet, Dzarongpu, sits at 16,500 feet and is one of the highest there. This photograph, taken by a Chinese geological expedition, shows the monastery with Mt. Everest in the background. Dzarongpu was the last stop for those attempting the Everest ascent from the Tibetan side.

At no time in its history was Buddhist monastic life meant to be a self-chosen process of world-forgetting and being by the world forgot. It was not . . . the purpose of a monastery to shut out the world, but only its distracting evils.

Sukumar Dutt
Buddhist Monks and Monasteries of India

When Tulshig Rimpoche came to Nepal, he reestablished his monastery among the Sherpas; local villagers helped his monk and nun followers build these new structures. Called Thupten Chöling Gompa, its name means a place of the Buddha's doctrine. (Any monastery is called *gompa* in Tibetan; *gom* means solitary place.) About one hundred monks and nuns practice here.

The monastery receives all manner of offerings from a widely scattered group of people. It serves a social function by distributing to the needy much of the food and clothing that it receives.

The large building in the center of the picture houses the images and provides space for services; it is appropriately called *lha khang*, or deity house, in Tibetan. The lama has his quarters in this structure. Off its main doors the *lha khang* has an enclosed courtyard surrounded by smaller buildings containing a kitchen, storage space, and a library. The individual houses scattered about the hill are those of the monks and nuns — monks to the left, nuns to the right. One, two, or even three people to a house, they are responsible for building their own quarters.

During a service Tulshig Rimpoche leads the chanting from his seat in the front of the *lha khang* altar. Services are held daily, and special days in the religious calendar are observed with the appropriate rites. Individuals may also arrange services that require the help of monks for funerals, ceremonies of meditational importance, or other special occasions.

Much that is circumstantial has now changed since the Buddha discovered and made known his liberating docrine 2500 years ago. . . . On the other hand, the Truth he discovered has remained untouched by all that circumstantial change. Old cosmologies give place to new; but the questions of consciousness, of pain and death, of responsibility for acts, and of what should be looked to in the scale of values as the highest of all, remain. Reasons for the perennial freshness of the Buddha's teaching — of his handling of these questions — are several, but not the least among them is its independence of any particular cosmology. Established as it is for its foundation on the self-evident insecurity of the human situation . . . [it] provides an unfailing standard of value, unique in its simplicity, its completeness and its ethical purity, by means of which any situation can be assessed and a profitable choice made.

Bhikkhu Ñāṇamoli
Preface to *The Path of Purification: Visuddhi Magga*

Tulshig Rimpoche receives people in his chambers for instructions or blessings. He returns the gift of a *katak*, or felicitous scarf, placing it around the neck of a devotee.

Friends exchange *kataks* on many occasions as an external symbol of their friendship. The student and teacher always meet as friends, regardless of any gulf between them in social status. The lama sees both the simple and the sophisticated. The exchange of the scarf might be a talisman for one or an abstract symbol for the other, but the gesture is the same for all.

Here Tulshig Rimpoche consecrates a painting, one intended to help the viewer strengthen his skills of perception. The deities depicted reflect some particular path to the understanding of illusion. The lama puts his thumb print on the back of the painting, behind each of the deities on the front. He also writes a note on the back to encourage the owner of the painting to see through delusion.

The teacher guides the student's efforts to become free from the beguilements of mere appearance. A painting, a carefully crafted image, can conform to the student's specific needs.

Mere painting can be done by anyone. The lama, or teacher, is empowered to put the "breath" into the deity. Even those who might not know the meaning of a particular deity can see the image and can partake of a certain spirit that the consecrated form imparts.

Besides being a community of over one hundred monks and nuns, Tulshig Rimpoche's monastery attracts many lay visitors who may need food, board, or an audience with the lama. The grounds and buildings also require maintenance. He is assisted in running this rather large organization by Ngawong Norbu, a very able and resourceful man who constantly invents ways of saving life's utensils from their destiny of becoming junk. For example, a length of wick pulled through a broken radio antenna was screwed into a bottletop, secured to the top of an attractive empty metal tea box, and suddenly became a new kerosene lamp. He applies these innovative skills to all of his administrative duties. His Tibetan title, *chagdzö*, means treasurer in English.

Chagdzö, as the highest office next to the lama, could be interpreted as a secular rank: the administrative arm of the religious leader representing a division of authority between religious and secular. This is not the case, however; the office of Chagdzö can be reached only by way of many years of training and study in the academic, artistic and administrative skills and their underlying religious principles and culture.

B. N. Aziz
"Views from the Monastery Kitchen"

Ngawong Tinley, a tall, thin monk, attends to the lama's personal requirements, serving the lama food and organizing his clothing. He has demonstrated extraordinary strength and compassion. Once on a trip to Kathmandu a nun traveling with him suffered from badly bruised feet. Ngawong Tinley thought nothing of carrying her on his back for five hours down a steep incline to the road. Here in the kitchen he assembles an offering plate, or *tsog*, for a service in progress in the *lha khang*.

A religious gathering, whether it is a monthly assembly or a permanent community, is for its members a community in which everyone is regarded with equal respect and accommodation; while each person retains his individuality and may enjoy his particular possessions and offices, there is a strong sense of sharing with and contributing to the work of the lama and to his selfless service of religion. This is symbolized in the tsog, the plate of offerings, which means literally: the group.
B. N. Aziz
"Views from the Monastery Kitchen"

We may gain insight into the vision of nonindustrial societies by looking at their rituals and festivals. The rhythms of traditional life conform to the seasons. The obvious cycles of sowing and reaping, summer and winter, and even youth and age provide a fleeting, and hence unsettling, glimpse of the world. Sherpas occasionally dip into eternity to make the mundane rhythms intelligible.

Once a year, in December, Tulshig Rimpoche travels to another monastery down the valley to officiate at a festival called Maṇi Rimdu. Similar festivals are celebrated throughout Tibet, but this particular one originated at Dzarongpu, where Tulshig Rimpoche's teacher, Ngawong Tenzin Norbu, composed and conducted its performance. The festival centers around a ceremony for long life and is preceded by a mystery play, which re-creates the introduction of Buddhism to Tibet. Sherpas are citizens of Nepal, not Tibet, but their culture reflects their Tibetan antecedents.

Tulshig Rimpoche rides a horse to this other monastery, known as Chiwong Gompa, established under the auspices of Ngawong Tenzin Norbu. Occasionally he meets villagers who seek his blessing, which he bestows by touching them with the bottom of a silver cylinder containing prayers.

What does living mean for a man who belongs to a traditional culture? Above all, it means living in accordance with extra-human models, in conformity with archetypes. . . . Living in conformity with the archetypes amounted to respecting the "law," since the law was only . . . the revelation . . . of the norms of existence, a disclosure by a divinity or a mystical being. And if, through the repetition of paradigmatic gestures and by means of periodic ceremonies, archaic man succeeded . . . in annulling time, he nonetheless lived in harmony with the cosmic rhythms; we could even say that he entered into these rhythms.

Mircea Eliade
The Myth of the Eternal Return: Cosmos and History

Monks in the Chiwong monastery courtyard play double-reed instruments, called *gyaling*, to herald Tulshig Rimpoche's arrival. When foreigners first hear Tibetan ecclesiastical music, the only description that comes to mind is cacophony. Because we bring an untrained ear to this music, we cannot immediately make sense of it. It is our ignorance of how to perceive these compositions, and not the musicians' inability to perform, that creates cacophony.

Just as they dismiss the music, outsiders can all too quickly judge festivals like Maṇi Rimdu as nonsense. In the same way we give up prejudices against unfamiliar music, we must surrender our preconceptions to appreciate the meaning of a mystery play.

The dance is accompanied by a recitation of the action that is being depicted and by a strange music which is undoubtedly suited to the evocation of a particular mood. . . . Whereas the layman sees in the dance or mystery play a representation of some historical event or other, it is possible on closer examination to discern that this is a secondary interpretation, behind which a very different meaning lies concealed. . . . The layman merely sees how, for example, a priest may acquire supernatural powers by winning influence over the demons and then "kills the evil king"; but the initiates understand that the whole action refers to the "killing of one's own self."

Peter H. Pott
"Tibet"

Monks on the rooftop and in the inner courtyard prepare to play long copper trumpets called *zang dung*. The inscription reads "May the glorious lama live forever." What does this mean? Nobody actually belives that the corporeal form of the lama endures forever. Since the lama's life embodies the Buddha's teaching, his body is seen as a symbol of this doctrine. This principle has no beginning or end and therefore is everlasting. Sherpas do not consider it paradoxical that an object with finite duration, like the body, coincides with the infinite.

As Tulshig Rimpoche enters, a young novice sounds the conch. This shell, here wrapped in a *katak*, the felicitous scarf, produces a penetrating sound.

The conch shell signifies the promulgation of the Buddha's precepts, or *Dharma*. The interior helix of the shell suggests the ever-renewing aspect of the universe, returning like a circle but always new and different. Any section of a helix intimates the furtherance of its own design. As this geometric pathway proceeds, the paradigm of the ideal teacher manifests itself in specific forms. All teachers in the Buddhist tradition consider themselves part of a lineage that extends infinitely in both past and future.

The conch shell was used in ancient India as a trumpet. It served in the army to transmit the orders of the officers to troops deployed in the field. At that time, it symbolized royalty and authority, i.e., sovereignty. It is but one step to the symbolism which was imposed on it by Brahmanism and later by Buddhism. In Brahmanism, the conch was one of the attributes most commonly used by divinities of Viṣṇuite origin. It became, in fact, the specific symbol of Viṣṇu, who used it, by virtue of the horrific sounds it emits, to spread terror among his enemies. As an attribute of this god, it is represented in the form of a simple shell. The use of the conch in Buddhism is only an adaptation of this earlier symbolism. Since the original use of the conch was the diffusion of the words of the commander to the armies of men, such was the case for its use as a Buddhist symbol, for here it signifies the spreading of the Law throughout the world.

E. Dale Saunders
Mudrā

Tulshig Rimpoche sits on a small porch immediately outside the *lha khang*. He overlooks the courtyard where the dances will take place. The perimeter of this courtyard has upper and lower galleries for the spectators.

The literal-minded Sherpa may venerate the flesh and opulence of the lama. The literal-minded foreigner may interpret all veneration this way. However, the allegorical-minded Sherpa interprets acts of respect on another level. The veneration becomes a reverence for the wisdom, potential or actual, that exists in both the lama and himself. Being privy to this exalted interpretation does not make him reluctant to pay his respects; instead, his understanding deepens the more frequently he performs the ritual. In societies in which ritual gesture has lost its value, people become mere custodians of exalted interpretations: they tend to think of the understanding of ritual as a substitute for its performance.

As the lama is welcomed in the main courtyard, a layman prepares offerings for the central altar. In pre-Buddhist Tibet, people offered animal sacrifices. The Buddhist moral code prohibits killing, so a substitute offering was devised — a dough cake made from toasted flour mixed with water. These *torma*, as they are called (or *gtor ma* as they are sometimes spelled), have a wide variety of shapes; they may be decorated with discs of cold butter. A wad of butter floats in the tub of water next to the completed *torma*.

An important object used in most ceremonies of the Tibetan clergy [is] sacrificial cakes, known as gtor ma. The gtor ma differ in shape, colour, and size according to the rite in which they are used and to which particular deity they are offered. The variety of gtor ma is therefore considerable, and a great number of learned Tibetan works has been devoted to this subject. Several of these texts give details about the manufacture of not less than one hundred eight different gtor ma. Some gtor ma are only a few inches high, while . . . the height of the so-called Kṣetrāpala'i gtor ma amounts to 10 ft. . . .

    Some of the gtor ma are simple cones bearing only a few ornaments, while others are complicated structures in the form of a palace, adorned with jewels, banners, flowers, etc., and representing the heavenly abode of the deity to which this particular gtor ma is dedicated, since in many ceremonies it is being assumed that the deity follows the call of the officiating priest and takes for some time residence in the gtor ma.

René de Nebesky-Wojkowitz
Oracles and Demons of Tibet

The mystery play begins with loud clashes of cymbals called *rolmo*. The ostensible story, the establishment of Buddhism in Tibet, describes an historical period. The mystery aspect of the play bespeaks a timeless process—an individual's awakening from illusion.

The first step in awakening is the transformation of perception. At the beginning of the play, an altar is built, where the objects of sensory perception are sacrificed. As if one purchases wisdom by spending the senses, one offers sound in the form of cymbals, taste in the form of dough cakes, smell in the form of burning juniper, touch in the form of silks, sight in the form of a mirror, and the mind in the form of a book. Freed from these patterns of material associations, one can perceive allegorical patterns.

The Greek root from which the word *mystery* stems means to close the lips or eyes. Mystery is not something you don't know; it's something you do know, but without the senses.

From inside the deity house of the monastery the next group of lamas emerges. They come to transform the indigenous beliefs of the people.

According to Tibetan histories, Buddhism came to that country in the first half of the seventh century A.D. The king at that time, Song-tsen Gam-po, had married both a Nepalese princess and a Chinese princess. He was attracted not only to these women, but also to the Buddhist practice they brought from their native countries. The Tibetans see him as a great civilizing figure who built their country's first Buddhist temples. Tibetan chronicles describe the period before his reign as dark and barbarous, and the arrival of Buddhist culture as light dispelling the darkness.

The decorative fire that tips the hats of the dancers' costumes represents this light, not material combustion. Buddhism conquered Tibet by uplifting, not by destroying.

Although the drama admits of an historical exposition, it also reflects an inner process. When greed, anger, or ignorance controls action, one's vision becomes clouded. When these three emotions, represented by the three skulls on the dancers' hats, pass away, vision becomes clear. Thus the fire suggests a process of illumination.

Victory breeds hatred. The defeated live in pain. Happily the peaceful live, giving up victory and defeat.

The Dhammapada

Buddhist Tibetans inherited the shamanic beliefs of their forebears. Still practiced in Siberia, shamanism may have been common to all the peoples of central and eastern Asia in ancient times. One feature of this practice is the shaman's ability to travel to other planes of existence in an ecstatic state. Often he travels by climbing a pole, which represents the axis of the world. These poles, which provide a juncture between the mundane world and the ecstatic realm, become a center about which the world revolves in shamanic rites. Although shamans actually climb such poles, the festival dancers use it as a focus about which they move.

When Buddhism came to Tibet, shamanism was not discarded or destroyed, but transformed by new ideas. In the older tradition, only the shaman could participate in the eternal; in Buddhism, everyone has this potential, not just the officiant.

The word for Buddhist in Tibetan is *nang-pa*, or interior person. One who does not share this interior emphasis is known as *chi-pa*, or exterior person. The shaman's flight becomes an interior journey, and ritual becomes an outward manifestation of an inward process. From their dance circle, the dancers briefly look within.

These masked dancers circle the courtyard with sprightly leaps. Called protectors of the faith, or *dharmapāla*, the origins of figures like these can be traced back to the pre-Aryan peoples of India. Originally known as *yakṣas* (literally, a wondrous thing), they were tree spirits, who were accepted by the Buddhists as defenders of the faith. In Nepal and Tibet, as in India, local deities were converted into protectors.

The history of Buddhism reveals the assimilation of many deities and beliefs already extant in countries where Buddhism penetrated. Over long periods a suitable niche was provided for many indigenous gods, as the deity's function became more clearly understood. The core of Buddhist teachings—the realization of the ephemeral quality of the self and its ultimate nonreality—gave these new interpretations a decidedly interior emphasis. Indigenous deities, converted from their previous roles as guardians of trees or springs, became *dharmapāla*, personal protectors of the channels leading inward.

A devotee of an alien sect devised a means to humiliate the Buddha and His disciples. The Buddha discovered it and succeeded in converting him to His Teaching. Due to lack of wisdom, the Buddha remarked, some could not realize the goodness of his disciples and He compared the ignorant to the blind and the wise to those who have eyes.

Nobody is condemned in Buddhism, for greatness is latent even in the seemingly lowliest just as lotuses spring from muddy ponds.

The Dhammapada

The moon is full, the fall harvest gathered, and people are at ease. Some have walked two or three days to come to the social event of the year. Farmers from warmer valleys sell peanuts and oranges outside the monastery walls, and people sitting in the lower galleries have shells and peels dropped from above onto their heads and shoulders. These groundlings frequently shout out to friends and dancers alike. The entire assemblage maintains a constant din, which forms an undertone for the performance.

A visitor might think the audience unable to fathom the psychological allegory of the drama. Indeed, few would be able to articulate their understanding of the play in sophisticated language; but comprehension should not be measured by verbal facility alone. Hardly any of these people bear the burdens of excessive anxiety or insecurity. Even the most naive Sherpas feel assured that any termination in life marks a new beginning; they are never overwhelmed by deadlines.

All wear their finest clothing. Women, whose habitual headgear is a towel, turn out in their best jewelry and most exquisite terrycloth.

In the dim light, a rare moment of quiet begins as everyone awaits the appearance of the star dancer to signify the firm establishment of the Buddha's teaching.

A solitary dancer appears, wearing a frightening blue mask and silk brocades. He represents Guru Rimpoche, sometimes called Padma Sambhava, a famous Indian teacher invited to Tibet around 770 A.D. The king, Tri-song De-tsen, asked him to instruct the people in techniques for dispelling illusion. Although an historically enigmatic figure, all accounts are unanimous in suggesting that he may have been the only person at that time capable of both subduing and illuminating the powerful shamanic tradition.

Tibetans respect Guru Rimpoche, whose name means precious teacher, as one of the most important figures in their history. Stories about Guru Rimpoche reveal his unusual ability to provide suitable instruction in diverse situations. Because of this ability to adapt, he is credited with eight manifestations. The dancer represents the one known as Dorje Drolo who carries a *phurba*, a three-edged spike that symbolically roots out the source of illusion, the belief in the self.

Nobody can maintain constant pious reverence for very long. Between the dances, almost as comic relief, this masked, bearded character and his straight man appear. Called Mi-tsering, or man of long life, he is popularly traced to a Chinese monk known as Ho Shang, who was defeated in a famous debate.

In this scene Mi-tsering explains all the intricacies of counting prayers on the rosary, or *mālā*, and exactly how one is to perform prostrations. His instructions are extremely exaggerated and all wrong, of course. He beats the daylights out of the poor everyman trying his best to learn. The crowd roars throughout their performance. It seems wisdom can be found through laughter as well as through piety.

After the dancing, Tulshig Rimpoche performs a ritual called the long-life ceremony, or *tse-wang*. At its culmination he passes out small red spherical pills with a palmful of sanctified wine and touches the heads of the participants in blessing.

The whole festival of Maṇi Rimdu takes its name from these red pills. *Rimdu*, in Sherpa, or *rildrup*, in Tibetan, means the ritual manufacture of medicinal pills. *Maṇi* means jewel; to Sherpas this word recalls the invocation, or mantra, "*Oṁ Maṇi Padme Hūṁ*." This epithet of the deity of compassion, Avalokiteśvara, means "He who holds the jewel and lotus." *Maṇi* represents the treasures and wealth associated with lucid vision; it corresponds to the philosopher's stone of the Europeans.

Far from being a placebo to prolong the body, the pills distributed at this long-life ceremony are intended to stimulate the decay of illusion. The superficial and temporary ego-identity masks the impregnable source of being, which has neither beginning nor end, as the ego does. Discovery of this source leads to immortality, certainly the longest life possible.

Eat this life pellet . . . consisting of the pure essence of the root of being manifested as living seed. . . . Eat it and may you receive the life-consecration of the unchanging adamantine mind.

Rin-chen gter-mdzod

Maṇi Rimdu lasts for three days; sleep is inevitable.

The wall painting depicts wisdom and the skillful means to employ it. Religious art is all symbolic; here the opposite poles of the universe are seen united as naturally as a father and mother. Indeed, the Tibetan term for united deities is *yab-yum*, and means precisely that—father-mother. Respect for one's parents is reinforced with such symbolism.

The mother represents wisdom, the space that provides for birth, the source of enlightening knowledge. The father is the skillful means, the embodiment of compassion. These two aspects of the absolute are seen in terms that sanctify a fact of life—the union of male and female—that is often a cause of embarrassment in many other cultures. Facts should never be causes of embarrassment or fear; only illusions cause uneasiness.

In dream there is neither the real object nor the senses to perceive [it], yet there is the perception; so also is the case with all our perceptions which we falsely take to be the direct copies of the thing itself.

Shashi Bhushan Dasgupta
An Introduction to Tantric Buddhism

An elderly nun who lives at Chiwong scurries to attend to her duties in the kitchen. Around her neck she wears a rosary, or *mālā* to count repetitions of *"Oṁ Maṇi Padme Hūṁ"* and other mantras. She suffers from an enormous goiter, a common malady among mountain dwellers who lack iodine in their diets.

Around three sides of the main temple building runs a passageway housing niches lined with prayer wheels. As the worshiper spins the wheels, *Oṁ Maṇi Padme Hūṁ*, printed endlessly on long strips of paper wound inside the cylinders, is carried out to all sentient beings.

The use of the forces of nature to turn wheels which generate energy for utilitarian purposes is a commonplace in our world, but only the Tibetans have produced wheels which are similarly rotated for purely spiritual purposes. The instrument [in this photograph is] rotated by hand; others are turned by wind and water power; and even the hot air which rises from the stove is often utilized to send forth blessings. As he rotates the wheel, the devotee should be aware that he is re-enacting the Buddha's turning of the Wheel of the Law, or setting in motion the doctrine.

Eleanor Olson
"The Meditations and the Rituals"

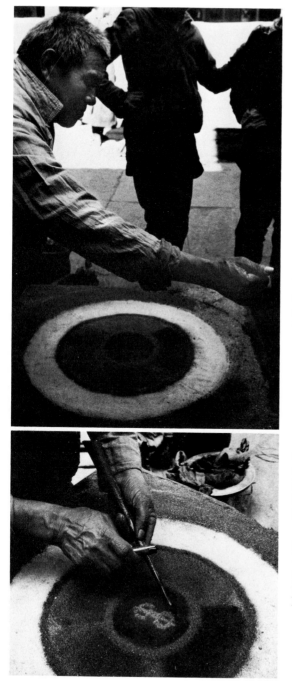

By the fourth day the long-life ceremony is complete, and everyone has some of its medicine. With farms in need of attention, most of the lay people return home; only a few remain. The lamas move to the courtyard and begin preparations for a sacrifice by fire.

Ang Chutu, the abbot of Chiwong monastery, uses colored sand to draw a diagram, or *mandala*, on a small pedestal. *Mandala* can mean circle or center. These figures have neither beginning nor end and thus allude to the timeless realm. Ritually, the *mandala* can serve as a ground where the limited and the unlimited interpenetrate. Although *mandalas* have enormously varied manifestations (they can be conceived as buildings, or can even be danced), they function as an opening to the centered, sacred, and transcendent. Therefore, they are used as aids to concentration and meditation.

The long metal cone holds colored sand. The serrations on the side produce a vibration when rubbed with a closed pocket knife, allowing the sand to pour out in a fine line through a little hole in the bottom.

In the center of the *mandala* is a sand-painted *dorje*, or diamond sceptre. The Tibetan *dorje*, or *vajra* in Sanskrit, is the symbol of the tantric school of Buddhism, found throughout Nepal, Tibet, China, Mongolia, Korea, Japan, and Indonesia.

Iconographically, the *vajra* can be traced to extreme antiquity. It grew out of the fertilizing lightning bolt of the male sky gods. This concept of incredible power was taken up by the tantricists, who produced an enormous literature on the meaning of this unique tool. They believe that emptiness, the substrate of phenomena, is the only constant in a cosmos so obviously subject to the laws of entropy. The self that is a thing, or the ego, decays. The *vajra* has come to suggest the immutable, awakened, empty self.

A monk completes a pyre constructed from kindling wood on top of the *maṇḍala*. The origins of this ceremony performed by the Sherpas can be traced to the practices of Vedic Indians, some three thousand years ago. In Vedic times, the motive for making an offering was to coerce a great sky god. The interpretation of this sacrifice has changed; Buddhists have transformed the act of purifying material objects into a therapeutic catharsis of the sacrificer, who asks for nothing in return.

When he officiates at the fire ceremony, Tulshig Rimpoche assumes the role of one who sacrifices without desire for repayment. Dressed as such a Bodhisattva figure, he wears a crown decorated with painted images of Buddhas representing five categories of wisdom, the *Jinas*.

A Bodhisattva acts without anticipation of reward and, motivated by compassion, stays among the unawakened to teach and lead. The Bodhisattva ideal is the hallmark of Mahāyāna Buddhism, practiced throughout central and northern Asia. The Bodhisattva delays his own release from illusion and maintains certain useful fictions to dwell among those still bound by the specter of ego. To delay one's own entrance into the supreme state, or *nirvāṇa*, for the sake of others is the ultimate gift and the ultimate state of desirelessness.

Bodhi means the highest knowledge. The word sattva in Sanskrit has different meanings, it means essence and it means determination . . . and also life. . . . The word bodhisattva may thus mean one whose essence, determination or life is the highest knowledge (bodhi).

Surama Dasgupta
Development of Moral Philosophy in India

These monks circumambulate the pyre after its ignition. One holds a long book wrapped in a felicitous scarf. The purifying fire takes the offerings and raises them toward the sky in smoke. In this particular case photographs of the body of a young Sherpa who had lost his life on a mountaineering expedition were added to the fire, and butter was poured over the flames. This circumambulatory ritual also recalls the way disciples showed respect for the Buddha's body.

The venerable Mahā Kassapa came to the Blessed One's pyre. . . . When he had done so, he arranged his robe on one shoulder, and raising his hands palms together, he circumambulated the pyre three times to the right. Then the Blessed One's feet were revealed, and he saluted the Blessed One's feet with his head. And the five hundred bhikkhus arranged their robes on one shoulder, and they did as the venerable Mahā Kassapa had done. But as soon as they had finished, the pyre caught alight of itself. And just as when butter or oil burns it produces neither cinder nor ash, so too in the burning of the Blessed One's body neither the outer skin nor the inner skin nor the flesh nor the sinews nor the oil of the joints produced any cinder or ash: only the bones remained.

Dīgha-nikāya

Tulshig Rimpoche holds the *vajra* to his breast with his right hand, and a bell with *vajra* handle in his left. The *vajra* symbolizes the skillful exercise of wisdom, which in turn is represented by the bell. Wisdom is not a thing that one knows and then parrots on occasion. Instead, it is seen as an openness that uses the circumstances of the moment to determine its expression. Buddhism has few dogmas; it expresses itself like an idiom using the most appropriate terms — what is true now will not be true later.

The bell stands for impermanence, an idea which underlies so much of Buddhist thought. "The sound which it emits is perishable; it is perceived but it may not be kept." The phenomenal world, then, is like the sound of the bell, "it is perceived, but it may not be kept." All things are perishable; they exist through the senses of the observer but have in themselves no reality. Like dew or the sound of a bell, they are transitory. So human life, similar to the ever-changing sounds of the bell, is changing, inconstant, unstable, pre-destined to that impermanence which is the essence of all things.

E. Dale Saunders
Mudrā

While Tulshig Rimpoche completes the ritual of sacrifice, Ngawong Tinley, his personal assistant, stands at his side. Although to one unacquainted with the hierarchical structure of Asian societies, the difference in social status between these two men might indicate inequality, both men regard social status as a fleeting and impermanent illusion. A person proves his substance through the selfless performance of his job, whatever it might be, rather than through his ability to switch jobs.

Regardless of the apparent disparity between the two, both Tulshig Rimpoche and Ngawong Tinley undertake this ritual of sacrifice, like all other tasks of life, with an equally selfless zeal. All participants in the sacrifice have a specific duty, and they try to perform their ceremonial responsibilities without thought of reward. Watching the fire consume the fruits of their work provides a visual confirmation of the dissolution of appearances.

The preceding service of purification consecrates the *maṇḍala* as the axis about which all things orbit—a still center unmodified by either time or space. Afterwards, the remaining villagers take handfuls of sand and ash from the destroyed *maṇḍala*. Because the mixture was charged at the transcendent source of the *maṇḍala*, it is believed to impart fecund powers to the fields and to protect dwellings.

Most Sherpas, their days filled by the demands of farming, rarely have the opportunity to dwell in the transcendent. However, those few who write the books that prescribe and interpret the dances, or who craft the images that grace the walls of monasteries and household altars, spend their days exploring that area where the mutable and the immutable interpenetrate.

VOCATION

Just above Gompa Zhung village sits another, smaller, monstery, named Serlo Gompa. Sangye Tenzin, the abbot here, is a Sherpa who studied for fifteen years in Kham, a province in eastern Tibet.

Many great Tibetan scholars studied in Kham. During the nineteenth century, the great Khampa lama Mipham (Mipham Jamyang Namgyal Rimpoche) was one of the major contributors to the Rimé movement, an attempt to integrate all schools of Tibetan Buddhism.

Philosophical studies in Mipham's own sect, the Nyingmapa, flourished. Like all Sherpa monasteries, Serlo is Nyingma, and the abbot, because of his studies in Kham, is in the direct lineage of Mipham.

Sangye Tenzin is a grammarian and logician. He has written the only history of the Sherpa people and the only grammar of the Sherpa language. He has won the respect of both Tibetan and Western Buddhist scholars.

Sangye Tenzin has a remarkable gift for creating conversations of astonishing clarity. He often finds examples from everyday life to illustrate principles of philosophy, taking care to tailor the example to fit the needs and proficiency of the questioner.

I once asked Sangye Tenzin why a Tibetan word, *tulwa*, meaning illusion, also describes the historical Buddha. He replied, "The real Buddha is like the sun, not only huge beyond our comprehension, but of a brilliance that is literally blinding. If we wish to examine the sun for any length of time, we can use its reflection in a small piece of colored glass. So it is with the Buddha. The fleshly body he assumes to appear among us only reflects what he really is."

Reality according to the Buddhists is kinetic, not static, but logic, on the other hand, imagines a reality stabilized in concepts and names. The ultimate aim of Buddhist logic is to explain the relation between a moving reality and the static constructions of thought.

T. Stcherbatsky
Buddhist Logic

Topgye, whose name means "great strength," is Sangye Tenzin's *chagdzö*, or treasurer. Here he stands beside a newly decorated prayer flag.

A man of great physical strength with the solid stance of a yak, he displays an unsuspected finesse in carving small graceful Tibetan letters on wooden printing blocks.

His great strength was once weakened by a devastating bout with a fever that lasted the better part of a month. While visiting to inquire about his health, I noticed several chickens squawking, scratching, and pecking about. This was quite extraordinary for this monastery, so I asked why they were there. Apparently Sangye Tenzin possesses a text describing the preparation of certain medicines indicated in protracted fevers, which specifies that certain animals, including chickens, must be liberated from the butcher's slaughtering block. Topgye recovered with no ill effects, and the chickens, deeply appreciative of their reprieve, spend their days in carefree abandon on a farm.

Tapkhay, "skillful means," and Ngawong Gendun, "authority of the monkhood," are two of Sangye Tenzin's students. Tapkhay, on the left, is a proficient woodblock carver. Ngawong Gendun is respected for being widely read in Tibetan literature; his eagerness to read has even led him to an investigation of English through the printing on the backs of wristwatches. This effort earned him the name "Unbreakable Mainspring" for many months.

Sangye Tenzin expects all of his monks to study the basic Buddhist canon — 108 volumes, divided into three parts: the *sutras*, or the words of the Buddha; the *abhidharma*, a psychological investigation; and the *vinaya*, or the code of behavior for the monkhood. This is the famous Tripiṭaka, or three baskets, found in varying editions in all Buddhist countries.

Tapkhay carves both words and images into wooden blocks that will be used for printing. The texts are volumes of the canon and its commentaries, as well as original compositions by his teacher, Sangye Tenzin. Here he works on a block depicting the wheel of life, or round of possibilities.

After consecration, the woodblock print assumes a vitality that influences observers, however unaware they may be. A text imparts even greater knowledge, as it forms a methodical explication of the philosophy. The supreme contact is, of course, meeting an enlightened individual. We cannot ask a book a question, we may not understand the meaning of an image, but interaction with one who practices what he advises can stimulate our own commitment to this advice.

Here, the carver's tools can be seen scattered about as he works on another block. They include slicers, gougers, and reamers, among others. Water-driven lathes shape the handles, and local smiths forge the tips of the tools. Metal sources include old truck springs, umbrella staves, and clock mainsprings. A neighboring village produces the paper for printing.

Plato identified (culture) with the capacity for immediate and instinctive discrimination between good and bad workmanship, of whatever sort; it is perhaps in this respect that the present age is least of all cultivated. We may expand this definition by including a certain quality of recollectedness or detachment, a capacity for stillness of mind and body (restlessness is essentially uncultured), and the power of penetrating mere externals in individual men or various races. Culture includes a view of life essentially balanced, where real and false values are not confused; also, I think, a certain knowledge or interest in things which are not directly utilitarian, that is to say, which do not merely give pleasure to the senses or confirm a prejudice. . . . Certain fine things which used to be obtainable in every market-place in the world are now only to be seen in museums. Because they are seen in museums, we imagine that we are cultured. . . . We know by their work that men of old were cultivated.

Ananda K. Coomaraswamy
Domestic Handicraft and Culture

87

Ngawong Gumbo, a farmer and carpenter, frequently turns his skill with wood to carving printing blocks. A disarmingly honest and genuine person, he has made several pilgrimages to central and western Tibet.

The hands of Ngawong Gumbo, toughened from the plough and the adze, carefully reveal the meaning of a text. When he carves woodblocks, he works at Thupten Chöling; many rely on his experience to correct grammatical errors or calligraphic renderings. Besides being a farmer, carpenter, and woodblock carver, Ngawong Gumbo is also a skillful cook and tailor. Such versatility is not unusual among the Sherpas.

Like many people in traditional societies, Ngawong Gumbo exhibits a reassuring self-confidence; one gets the feeling he can learn and do anything well. As he huddles by a window in his woolen robes, the penetrating cold of late fall doesn't seem to affect the dexterity of his fingers. Concentrating on the task at hand, he appears to have lost himself in his work. It may very well be his ability to lose himself that makes him so deft.

Ang Gelbu, like his teacher Lama Sangye Tenzin, has also studied in the eastern Tibetan province of Kham. In those earlier days, he had been a monk; now a layman, he too carves woodblocks. Here his skilled eye reads the type, carved in its mirror image, checking for errors.

Donations were collected to carve a set of blocks and reprint a philosophical commentary by Mipham. Sangye Tenzin had brought back a copy of this rare book from Kham. His students were devoting their time and carving skills to this ambitious undertaking.

The sign behind Ang Gelbu is in the Nepali language, which uses the Devanagari alphabet, the same as that used for some Indian languages. The Tibetan alphabet, although different, is based on similar phonetic principles. The Tibetans claim not to have had an alphabet prior to the introduction of Buddhism. Their letters now are based on a Gupta dynasty script used during the eighth century in northern India.

A large printing job requires the preparation of huge vats of ink, which the Sherpas generally make from pine soot. This ink may be used both in painting and in woodblock printing. An inverted biscuit tin is placed above the fire to collect the smoke residue. The particles of soot are removed from the tin and bound together with a small amount of animal-skin glue, generally made from the cow, or from the cow-yak cross, the *zopkio*. There are no butchers here, but not infrequently an animal loses its footing on the precarious cliffs where it grazes. When this happens, the flesh is consumed and the skin is used to make glue for painters and printers.

It's hard to imagine a dingier job than blending soot and glue. Yet this man's service in dealing with the opaque ink can help produce lucid insights in a reader.

Simply calling to mind what the city or the house, nature, tools, or work have become for modern man and non-religious man will show with the utmost vividness all that distinguishes such a man from a man belonging to any archaic society, or even from a peasant of Christian Europe. For modern consciousness, a physiological act — eating, sex, and so on — is in sum only an organic phenomenon. . . . But for the primitive, such an act is never simply physiological; it is, or can become, a sacrament, that is, a communion with the sacred. . . .

Sacred and profane are two modes of being in the world, two existential situations assumed by man in the course of his history.

Mircea Eliade
The Sacred and the Profane: The Nature of Religion

The Solu valley has nurtured several accomplished painters, men who paint the monastery walls and furnishings and, most important, produce the famous scrolls of Tibetan Buddhists, called *tankas*. *Tankas* are almost always individually commissioned; they are not decorative art, but act as a key to unlock specific illusions that may bind the viewer of the *tanka*. A person performing meditations that include the visualization of deities may commission a *tanka*, as may someone who requires an image for the services prescribed by his teacher. An important lama commissions a wide variety of *tankas*, often intended to illustrate his meditative experience.

Every Sherpa home has an altar, for which a family orders images according to its financial capabilities. The least expensive image, of course, is a woodblock impression on local paper. Equating the sacred with a specific amount of cash or goods is considered inappropriate, however, so the patron gives the painter a suitable gift in return for the *tanka*, the value of the gift depending on the patron's means. Everyone always seems pleased after this exchange of gift and *tanka*.

This man is Kaba Danu, one of the youngest of the Solu painters. A married layman, he has three children. Here he works on a *mandala*.

One of Kaba Danu's finished works known as the *Sipé Khorlo*, or the "round of possibilities," illustrates states of mind. Each sector of the wheel represents a world, or a particular state of mind. Within a single day the mind can range through all of these states, according to the degree of discomfort or pleasure one may experience. We desire to experience pleasure; we become angry when we do not; and we are unaware of this interplay of emotion. These three principles—ignorance, desire, and anger—represented by the pig, the cock, and the snake chasing each other in the hub of the wheel, govern our movements through the mind states. At the top and slightly to the right, is a standing Buddha pointing away from this wheel, indicating that equanimity is not found through these transmigrations.

Said the king: "Reverend Nāgasena, is the person who is reborn the same person, or a different person?"
Said the Elder: "He is neither the same person nor a different person." "Give me an illustration." . . .

What do you think about this, great king? You are now big. You were once young, tender, weak, lying on your back. Are you the same person now that you were then?

No indeed, Reverend Sir. He that was young, tender, weak, lying on his back was one person; I, big as I am now, am a different person. . . .

Suppose, great king, some man or other were to light a lamp. Would that lamp burn all night long?—Yes, Reverend Sir, it would burn all night long.

Well, great king, is the flame that burns in the first watch the same as the flame that burns in the middle watch?—No indeed, Reverend Sir. . . .

Well, great king, was the lamp one thing in the first watch, something different in the middle watch, and something still different in the last watch?—No, indeed, Reverend Sir. The lamp was only the cause of the flame that burned all night long.

"Precisely so, great king, there is an uninterrupted succession of mental and physical states. One state ceases to exist and another comes to exist. The succession is such that there is, as it were, none that precedes, none that follows. Thus it is neither that same person nor yet a different person which goes to the final summation of consciousness." . . .

"You are a clever man, Reverend Nāgasena!"

Milindapañha: Questions of Milinda

Kaba Par Gyaltsen, another Solu painter, lives in a very small settlement, only a twenty-minute walk from Thupten Chöling, Tulshig Rimpoche's monastery. Both Kaba Par Gyaltsen and Kaba Danu, who lives five hours down the valley, studied with Kaba Puri, a famous Sherpa painter of the 1940s. Kaba Par Gyaltsen supplemented this study with a stay at Tashi Lhunpo monastery in Shigatse, Tibet.

Kaba, in Sherpa, comes from the Tibetan *khepa*, and means clever or learned. The Sherpas use this word almost exclusively as an appellation for painters. A painter usually has a good grasp of the enormous variety of icons involved in the tantric, or vajrayāna, sect of Buddhism, and this alone deserves respect. Curiously, however, it is considered that no amount of knowledge itself, whether it be of iconography or even of literature or philosophy, has any correlation with wisdom. Stories abound of totally unlettered, but nonetheless enlightened, people.

Kaba Par Gyaltsen lives with his wife and seven children in this rather modest house (though a close look at the picture reveals a few of the children off playing). His lot is a difficult one, as the size of his family might suggest.

He works mostly for the lamas, who provide his household necessities. Few Sherpas are deeply involved with the cash economy. He and Kaba Danu, the other major lay painter of Solu, cultivate land and raise wheat, barley, potatoes, and some greens, which help enormously in sustaining the family.

Although Kaba Par Gyaltsen and his family project an air of formality for the camera, they project warm hospitality to a human being, offering buttered tea from the Sherpas' ubiquitous thermos. I once told him of a news item concerning the efficiency of a thermos device developed for the American space program. This device was reportedly capable of maintaining beverages at a piping hot temperature for 2000 years. Kaba Par Gyaltsen's entire face curled in hilarity as he asked, "Who's going to drink it, the immortals?"

Almost everything an artist uses is of local manufacture. Here Kaba Par Gyaltsen makes a brush. Sticks for the shaft are easy to come by in a forest, although some painters prize imports, especially the red, or blood, sandalwood from India.

The shaft is sharpened to a point; a very small notch girds the beginning of the taper. The hairs for this fine-tipped brush come from the jungle cat, a kind of lynx. For brushes used in the application of color, rather than line, the cheek hairs of a goat work admirably. The hairs are first aligned in a small bamboo joint and the painting ends glued together with ash and water soluble glue. After this has dried the other end is clipped straight across, and the whole affair is fit around the taper of the brush handle, secured with wet glue, and straightened with another "blank" brush.

A loop of thread is tied firmly to the tip of the taper, about halfway into the hairs.

104

The short end of the loop is then held parallel to the shaft, and the longer end is wound down to the ledge previously carved. These two ends are tied. Next, the adhesive and ash in the tip hairs are washed out.

Kaba Par Gyaltsen inspects the tip, picking off errant hairs to make it perfect. A few of the painters have been introduced to plastic glue, excellent for securing the windings of thread since it is not water soluble. But plastic glue, although efficient, is hardly necessary.

As the brush takes shape, Kaba Par Gyaltsen comments on its role in the artist's work: "Brushes are like little gods. In fact, you should think of them all as the sword of Manjusri, the patron deity of our craft. You should never put a brush in your mouth as it's disrespectful. Always keep them in a high place and never allow them to fall to the floor."

Tulshig Rimpoche recently added a new library wing to his monastery, and he commissioned Kaba Par Gyaltsen to preside over the painting of murals for it. These murals are often called frescoes, but the appellation is misleading. Sherpas and Tibetans paint on a dry surface, not on wet plaster as the Italian *buon fresco* suggests.

Kaba Par Gyaltsen bends over a brazier holding paint pots. The paint must be kept warm, as the glue congeals quickly in the cold air.

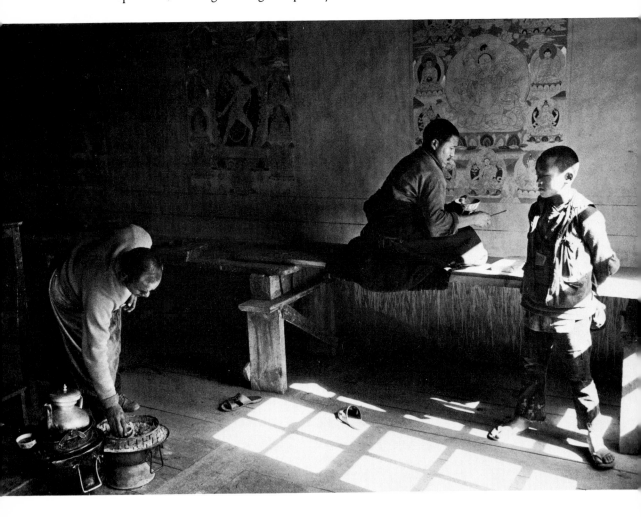

The growing interest in Tibetan sculpture and painting nowadays is clearly due as much to their religious subject-matter as to their aesthetic value. What is known to us of these arts is almost exclusively religious. . . . The painters and sculptors . . . are regarded as humble craftsmen, and not as individual creators. Apart from a few monks, remembered for reasons unconnected with their art, only a few obscure names have been preserved for us, on fifteenth-century frescoes. The Tibetans tell us nothing, throughout their history, of any eminent painter, any remarkable or famous work of art, nor are their paintings and sculptures ever signed. . . .

We should not conclude that the products of these craftsmen fall short of being works of art, for all their creators' humility and religious preoccupations. Tibetans are certainly capable of evaluating the quality or execution of a work aesthetically. But it is above all the religious subject they are interested in. So we miss the whole point, of some of the paintings, at any rate, if we admire composition and colors that are not due to the painter's free choice but imposed on him by textbooks of ritual. The mandalas, for instance, whose well-ordered symmetry would delight a town-planner, are likely to give the European beholder an impression of stylistic elegance or an aesthetic satisfaction that were not intended by the artist, and are not felt by a Tibetan audience. It is the same with the colours, gestures, and attributes of various deities which are all carefully laid down in books.

The reason for this dependence on ritual texts is that pictorial representation is a religious act, in the same way as mental creation when meditating. . . . It is this process which explains the proliferation of iconographic variants on a single subject. Meditative creation is manifold by its very nature, and is reflected in poetic or artistic creation.

R. A. Stein
Tibetan Civilization

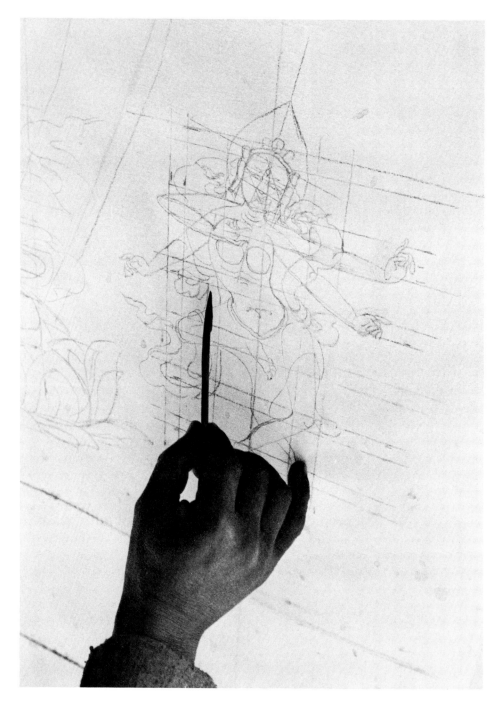

The lama gives a schematic diagram for every wall. Kaba Par Gyaltsen then draws out each deity with charcoal, according to the canonical proportions prescribed by the texts.

Contemporary artists in the West may view canonically prescribed art forms as antiquated and stifling. Any artist must follow the rules dictated by his particular style; freedom is found within these rules.

Just as conscience is externalized in rules of conduct, or the principles of thought in logic, so aesthetic pramana [the norm of properly conceived design] finds expression in rules . . . , or canons of proportion. . . . The gambolling of lambs, however charming, is not yet dancing.

Ananda K. Coomaraswamy
The Transformation of Nature in Art

With the sketch completed, the colors are blocked in. Sherpas praise highly any work done in a monastery. Monks, nuns, and lay people are all eager to help on monastery projects. Although not a painter by profession, this monk applies color enthusiastically.

The physical union with a feminine partner described and formed as Śakti should not only symbolize attainment of the highest union but can also be employed as a method of reaching the desired loss of identity. It should be quite clear what problems are posed by this, and also the extent to which the direction of an experienced teacher is necessary to preserve the requisite or desired separation between symbol and reality.

Peter H. Pott
"Tibet"

Kaba Par Gyaltsen and his eldest son, Ang Phurba, letter a prayer wheel with *Oṁ Maṇi Padme Hūṁ*, the invocation of the deity of compassion, Avalokiteśvara. If funds were available, such lettering would be done in gold. Here, however, powdered brass substitutes. Brass generally lasts for three or four years before it turns black.

The gold painting fades when it is completed—
This shows the illusory nature of all beings,
This proves the transient nature of all things.
Think, then, you will practice Dharma.

Milarepa
The Hundred Thousand Songs of Milarepa

Another type of work occasionally required of a painter is to make a tracing of an extant, and often old, *tanka*. This particular painting had been done by a previous incarnation of Tulshig Rimpoche, and a copy was needed for a lama in Darjeeling. Tracing paper from India was laid over the top, and the entire image was copied with brush and ink. It is then possible, although it was not required in this case, to prick small pin holes along all of the ink lines, place the tracing paper on a piece of sized stretched cotton, and rub the entirety with a porous rag filled with powdered charcoal. *Tsigpar*, as this stencil is called, provides a simple way of producing a pattern, which can then be inked and colored in the usual manner.

The nearest power line is some five days distant from Tulshig Rimpoche's monastery, so work like this is usually done during the daylight hours. The importance of light is impressed upon the foreign observer, who frequently takes light for granted. Here the contrast between daylight and darkness permits a rare excitement to build. The development of a painting sees conscious attention flood the surface of the work during the day and subliminal attention percolate at night. The images grow like little flowers, opening and closing with the sun.

Kaba Par Gyaltsen visits a Sherpa monk who is also a painter. His name is Ngawong Lekshi, more familiarly, Au Leshi, or Uncle Leshi. (*Lekshi* translates as "good speech" and is comparable to the name Benedict.) A most unusual individual, he has been a monk since the age of twelve. Now in his mid-sixties, Au Leshi has removed himself from the monastery to live out his days in the forest.

Au Leshi's little house is perched on the side of a cliff, tucked under a large boulder overhang. He refers to this residence as his cave; within its precincts he has a surprising number of refinements. The faucet delivers water from a dammed-up trickle found farther up the cliff; directly beneath the faucet, a trap door permits drainage to tumble down the rock face. The cooking pot sits on an incredibly efficient stove fashioned from empty biscuit tins.

There is no bed. He sleeps cross-legged and erect in the same place where he reads, eats, and paints.

Upon leaving the monastery (he had been at Thupten Chöling), Au Leshi took a vow never to cross another's threshold. He retired to a spot where his father had had a retreat. The previous structure having long since vanished into the maw of time, he set up a small tent. This was shelter enough to sit upright for meditation, but provided room for only one.

He had one small cooking pot, but no store of grain or garden to harvest. The forest, if you know what you are doing, proves an endless source of food. There are stinging nettles (a delicacy in French cuisine), wild tubers, and even a cliff-growing plant that is slightly sour to serve as a pickle. Au Leshi lived on these for several months, just as his father and countless other men and women before him had done. Then a woodcutter chanced upon him. Sherpas respect one who foregoes the pursuit of material goods and accepts what is provided. News of the hermit's presence on the side of a steep cliff near the village of Gompa Zhung, brought pious visitors with offerings, though he asked for nothing.

Two young monks in their twenties, studying at Serlo monastery, heard of Au Leshi's cave, as it came to be known, and asked if he would teach them. As the tent was not large enough to accommodate three, they offered to build a more permanent structure onto the face of the rock cliff. As more students sought instruction, additions were made.

(He was) one who, having had the advantage of holy and sacred teachers, stored up the life-giving elixir that fell from their lips, and tasted it for himself in the delightful solitude of mountain retreats, thereby obtaining emancipation from the toils of Ignorance, (so that) the seeds of Experience and Inspiration sprouted up in him and attained to full growth.

Rechung
Jetsün-Kahbum: Biography of Milarepa

Many think that Au Leshi's life is exemplary. From time to time people come to him requesting blessings, memorial services, or just plain advice. Frequently people ask for a small painting.

Traditionally, a hermit like Au Leshi has a public room. A small aperture, opening on another room of the hermitage, provides the only way to view and speak with the lama. When Au Leshi receives guests in this public room, they approach the window, deferentially lower their heads, and offer him a small gift wrapped in a felicitous scarf. People who have money may give him a little, those who don't may give butter or wheat. When the people leave, or if he is tired, the little door to the public room closes.

When the Buddhist ascetic goes into seclusion (restrains the sense door), it would be incorrect to say of him that he "leaves the world"; for where a man is, there is his world. . . . So when he retreats from the clamour of society to the woods and rocks, he takes his world with him, as though withdrawing to his laboratory, in order the better to analyse it.

Bhikkhu Ñāṇamoli
Introduction to *The Path of Purification: Visuddhi Magga*

The act of painting occupies a large part of Au Leshi's time. Ideally the image maker identifies with the wisdom represented by the deity during every stage of the work. This emphasis on the interior quality of exterior creations is what delineates sacred art from idolatry.

At this stage a rectangle of cotton cloth has been sewn onto four bamboo strips. These, in turn, are laced around the inside of a heavier wooden frame. A solution of glue and zinc oxide (in Tibet, chalk) is applied in successive coats to fill the space of the fabric and to create a smooth surface upon which to paint. Between each coat the fabric is rubbed smooth.

"You know what this is?" he asks. "It is the *prajñāpāramitā*," the great mother, emptiness, infinite potential out of which comes the deity.

Forms are not wisdom, nor is wisdom found in form,
In consciousness, perceptions, feeling, or in will.
They are not wisdom, and no wisdom is in them.
Like space it is, without a break or crack.

Of all objective supports the essential original nature is boundless;
Of beings likewise the essential original nature is boundless.
As the essential original nature of space has no limits,
Just so the wisdom of the World-knowers is boundless.

Prajñāpāramitā-Ratnaguṇasamcayagātha:
Verses on the Perfection of Wisdom

He rubs with a broken piece of conch shell—an appropriate instrument as the *tanka*, like the conch, propounds the teaching of the Buddha. He says that our minds are usually distracted; we are unaware of what we do. Each step in the creation of a painting provides an opportunity to concentrate on what is happening. Study offers the same opportunity to scholars. However, painters do not necessarily take advantage of this opportunity any more than scholars take advantage of theirs. An artist may be able to create an image of the Buddha, and a scholar may be able to defeat all comers in debate. Concentration, however, requires an ineffable interior transformation, independent of artistic or logical skills.

127

In an effort to convey to Au Leshi that I too was privy to the secrets that artists hold, I once parroted a phrase that I had heard a friend, a talented American painter, say: "You know, all painting is in the eye." "No, you're wrong," Au Leshi said. He pointed out that a dead man might have eyes that are "in perfect working order" and yet he does not see. "The sight, and skills in perception, are here," and he pointed to his breast. "The eye is no more than a window."

People say: 'My mind was elsewhere; I did not see. My mind was elsewhere; I did not hear. It is with the mind, truly, that one sees. It is with the mind that one hears. Desire, imagination, doubt, faith, lack of faith, steadfastness, lack of steadfastness, shame, meditation, fear — all this is truly mind. Therefore even if one is touched on his back, he discerns it with the mind.'

Bṛhad-Āraṇyaka Upanishad

The nature of this mystery dwelling in the breast is the most important part of what Au Leshi wishes to teach his student. Many people believe that the perceptive faculty resides in the head. But most people instinctively point to their breasts when surprised, and say something like "Who, me?" The heart generates both concentration and distraction.

Desire, for example, can often interfere with concentration. If the heart is affixed to some attractive image in fantasy, perception of the present moment is impaired. These clouding emotions are often called poisons; they all have antidotes, and both poison and antidote arise from within. To search for this source is literally the heart of the matter. Painting for Au Leshi is precisely this practice of searching for the source and discovering the wise stroke.

The maker of an icon, having by various means proper to the practice of Yoga eliminated the distracting influences of fugitive emotions and creature images, self-willing and self-thinking, proceeds to visualize the form of the devatá, angel or aspect of God, described in a given canonical prescription. . . . The mind "pro-duces" or "draws" . . . this form to itself, as though from a great distance. Ultimately, that is, from Heaven, where the types of art exist in formal operation; immediately, from "the immanent space in the heart" . . . , the common focus . . . of seer and seen, at which place the only possible experience of reality takes place.

Ananda K. Coomaraswamy
The Transformation of Nature in Art

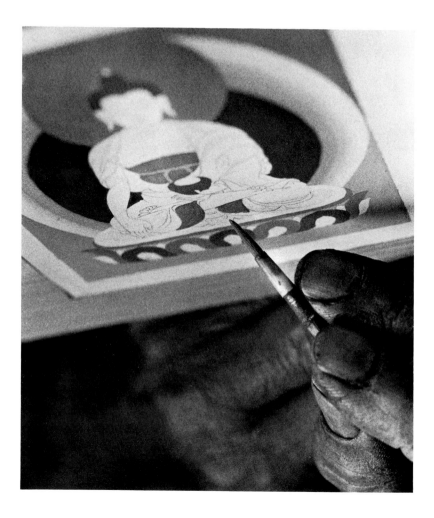

The more you talk about It, the more you think about It, the further from It you go;
Stop talking, stop thinking, and there is nothing you will not understand.
Return to the Root and you will find the Meaning;
Pursue the Light, and you will lose its source,
Look inward, and in a flash you will conquer the Apparent and the Void.
For the whirligigs of Apparent and Void all come from mistaken views;
There is no need to seek Truth; only stop having views.

Seng-ts'an
On Trust in the Heart

Au Leshi's brush details a small image of the historical Buddha. The image evoked in an artist's heart passes through his hand to the outside world. One must practice seeing clearly with the heart before one can draw from it. The paths of artist and sage, which intertwine in Au Leshi's life, can be recognized in the life of the Buddha, in which sagacity came with perception.

About the sixth century B.C. a prince of northern India found no satisfaction in his fortunate surroundings. One's material acquisitions have little influence on the fate of sickness, old age, and death that both rich and poor suffer. He studied with a variety of men proficient in the philosophical systems of those times, but no one could explain the reason for this fate. Finally he left his companions and vowed to remain sitting under a tree until he found the source of dissatisfaction. And there, in quiet meditation, he found the answer in himself, not in a system. *Budh*, in Sanskrit, means to understand or awaken; *buddha* means awakened; so from this point on, he was called the Buddha. The Buddha is the foundation of all the myriad of deities in the lamaist pantheon. All represent parts of the awakened mind and therefore are not worshiped, but discovered within oneself. One need only understand one deity to understand all the rest.

We all doubt; at times we are all uncertain. Uncertainty, or ignorance, gives rise to an unsatisfactory state. If our situation is unsatisfactory, and we don't understand why, then we want something else. If the desire is not satisfied, then anger follows accordingly: "Why can't I have. . . ." From this naturally comes arrogance: "I deserve. . . ." The last step is jealousy: "Why should anyone else. . . ." The wisdoms that counteract these poisons—ignorance, desire, anger, arrogance, and jealousy—form the most common pentad of deities in the lamaist tradition.

Au Leshi admonishes us to be constantly alert for the arising of any of these poisons, and to jump at their source quickly. For an answer we must look not outside of us, but to the heart of the problem.

A compass of bamboo staves describes a halo as Au Leshi asks, "Do you know the difference between a lion and a dog? If you throw stones at a dog, he will follow the stones. You can drive a dog away from you with stones. Now if you throw stones at a lion, he will immediately go to the source of the stones. The stones are greed and anger; be a lion!" When we experience desire or anger, he says we should ask ourselves, "Where does it come from? What shape is it? What color? Look to their source—ask yourself, 'Where is the mind? Where is the heart?'"

134

If anger that dwells in our heart lies neglected
  And, turning instead to our external foes,
We try to destroy them and even kill thousands,
  Then thousands of others will plague us still more.
So seeing this action is not the solution,
  Let's muster the forces of mercy and love;
Turn inwards and tame the wild flow of our mind-stream—
  The Sons of the Buddhas all practise this way.

Indulging in objects our senses run after
  And drinking salt water are one and the same;
The more we partake, for our own satisfaction,
  The more our desire and thirst for them grow.
Thus when we conceive a compulsive attraction
  Towards whatever object our senses desire,
Abandon it quickly without hesitation—
  The Sons of the Buddhas all practise this way.

Thogs-med bzang-po
Thirty-seven Practices of All Buddhas' Sons

Applying detail to the Western Paradise of Amitābha Buddha, Au Leshi says, "Of course, they say that faith will put you there after death, but a total absence of greed will do the very same thing while still alive here on earth. There are people among us who have done it." Amitābha's paradise is said to have streets of gold, and anything you want appears. From another perspective, if you don't want anything, everything is gravy.

The imperial delegate paid reverence and asked again, "I observe that monks, disciples who have renounced their families, and lay folk always recite the name of Amitābha with the hope of going to and being reborn in the Western Region (Pure land, Paradise). Will your Holiness explain whether it is possible to be born there or not? Please remove my doubts."

The Great Master [Hui-neng, the sixth patriarch] said, "Imperial Delegate, please listen. I will explain it to you. According to the scripture spoken by the World-honored One in Śrāvastī about leading people to the Western Region, it is quite clear that it is not far from here. It is said to be far away for the benefit of people of low intelligence, but it is said to be near for the benefit of people of high intelligence. People are of two kinds, but the Law is only one. Because men differ according as they are deluded or enlightened, some understand the Law quicker than others. Deluded people recite the name of the Buddha hoping to be born in the Pure Land, but the enlightened purifies his own mind, for, as the Buddha said, 'As a result of purity of mind, the Buddha Land becomes pure.' . . . One has only to be straightforward in his actions and he will reach the Pure Land in a moment. . . . What is the need for wanting to go and be born there?"

The Platform Scripture

What is a Buddhist? *Budh* in Sanskrit means to awake, to understand, so a Buddhist is simply one who seeks an awakening, regardless of the system. Indian Buddhism consisted largely of dogmas molded out of the Buddha's awakened attitudes to extant Hindu philosophies. Every country that Buddhism entered had an indigenous religion. Buddhism affirmed that religion and built on it. In China it was Taoism and Confucian thought; in Japan it was Shintoism; in Tibet it was shamanism. The contribution of Buddhism was an understanding, an awakened attitude. The resulting varied expressions of Buddhism appear to differ in details such as which texts are emphasized, what color robes the monks and nuns wear, and what kind of face is chiseled on the Buddha images, yet the different branches of Buddhism have a common root. This source, a faceless understanding, can attach itself to any system and vitalize it. When Guru Rimpoche brought Buddhism to Tibet, he did not destroy the local deities but used them to protect the Buddha's teaching. Many of the wrathful aspects of the Tibetan Buddhist pantheon are derived from precisely these pre-Buddhist sources. They serve to frighten those who would thwart the process of dispelling illusions.

Au Leshi seems interested in discovering the spirit of truth in every faith, and in this way he remains faithful to the tradition of the awakened and not to dogmas. To illustrate, he once spoke of the stereotypes of Hindu and Moslem philosophies: "You know, a Hindu will pray to all sorts of images, even to rocks and trees. A Hindu can find the self, or Atman, in substance. A Moslem will pray to no images whatsoever; God, or Allah, is completely empty. An awakened person, however, is always involved in the subtle interplay of the self and emptiness."

There is a science of theology, of which Jewish, Christian, Hindu and Muslim theology are only special applications. It is just as if we were to discuss mathematics with an Oriental scholar; we should not have in mind the mathematics of white or colored men as such, but only the mathematics itself. In the same way, it is not about your God or his God that you must learn to talk with the Oriental theologian, but about God himself.

Ananda K. Coomaraswamy
"A Lecture on Comparative Religion"

Au Leshi's painting is of the teacher who established Buddhism in Tibet, Guru Rimpoche, whose name means most precious teacher. One figure may be represented in several different ways, depending on which aspect of his work is to be emphasized. Here, Guru Rimpoche appears as Padma Sambhava, which means the one born from a lotus. Often a central image will be surrounded by figures significant in his history. Teachers, consorts, and deities surround Guru Rimpoche in an arrangement designed for contemplation.

The colors, all water soluble, are mainly synthetic poster colors from India and Japan. Before the 1950s mineral colors ground from stones were brought from Tibet and China. Au Leshi has a personal cache of these better colors for commissions from important lamas, but these works are very rare today. Many current commissions are for use in funeral services.

The King, Thī-Srong-Detsan, who reigned from A.D. 740 to 786 . . . invited Padma-Sambhava to Tibet to help in the re-establishment of Buddhism. . . . He supervised the building of the first Buddhist monastery in Tibet, that at Sāmyé, overthrew the ancient ascendency of Tibet's shamanistic pre-Buddhist religion known as the Bön (or Bön-po), and firmly established the Tantric or deeply esoteric form of Tibetan Buddhism. As a direct result of Padma-Sambhava's efforts, the people of Tibet were elevated from a state of barbarism to a state of unsurpassed spiritual culture. He is, therefore, truly one of the greatest of the World's Culture Heroes.

His less critical devotees generally regard the strange stories told of him . . . as being literally and historically true; the more learned interpret them symbolically. And the anthropologist observes that the historic Padma-Sambhava, like the historic King Arthur, is barely discernible amidst the glamour of legend and myth.

W. Y. Evans-Wentz
The Tibetan Book of the Great Liberation

141

Au Leshi painted this *tanka* many years ago. The quality of the colors is unlike that of any others to be seen in Solu, or indeed anywhere in Nepal or India in my experience. When questioned about this *tanka*, Au Leshi replied that it had been done during a six-year retreat on a high mountain pass. He had little food, let alone colors, so he used vegetable dyes derived from a nearby forest.

The painting itself depicts Lab-kyi Dron-ma. An historical figure of the twelfth century, she has become a popular icon among Tibetans. She married and had four or five children, who are scattered on the row beneath her in the painting. Like their mother, they all contributed to Tibetan Buddhist culture. Lab-kyi Dron-ma was one of the earliest Tibetan adepts of a practice called *chöd*. Literally meaning to cut off, *chöd* aims at cutting off one's belief in the ego.

The *chöd* rite is performed alone, often in a remote area. The practitioner sanctifies the ground by dancing a *mandala* to the five directions. The center purifies the practitioner of negligence; the west, of greed; the east, of anger; the south, of arrogance; and the north, of jealousy. After this purification, a ritual is performed which severs the basis of ego, the desire for a separate, sensuous existence. The ritual of cutting instantaneously identifies the practitioner with alert, nonillusory perception and ends alienation.

Chöd is one of the most demanding, both physically and psychologically, of all yogic exercises. Here deities involved in the practice, and other practitioners, surround the central figure of Lab-kyi Dron-ma.

Why protect it, O Mind? Why treat the body as one's own? If it is apart from you, then what to you is its decay?

You would not foolishly take as your own a filthy wooden doll. Why should I protect a stinking machine made of excrement?

By full use of the imagination take apart this leather bellows. With the knife of wisdom (prajñā) cut the flesh from a cage of bone.

Then, having taken apart the bones, behold the marrow within, and ask yourself, "Where is its essence?"

Moreover, having searched carefully, and having seen that there is no essence of yourself, now you ask, "Why should I still protect the body?"

Śāntideva
Bodhicaryāvatāra: Entering the Path of Enlightenment

Au Leshi usually gets up at three in the morning and reads scriptures until around six. He then has a service for all the beings of the world. This service is intended to relieve the suffering of men, animals, gods, and hell creatures, all of whom represent states of mind through which we pass during the course of a day, or hour, or minute. Each action of the ritual can be performed with perfunctory automation or with concentration. By examining the emotional states every morning, and trying to be aware of them throughout the day, Au Leshi further relaxes his grasp on the selfish ego. His hands are raised in a gesture of teaching, directed to others who may be unaware of their emotional states.

The best method of acquiring Wisdom is unfaltering endeavour.
The Ocean of Delight for the Wise

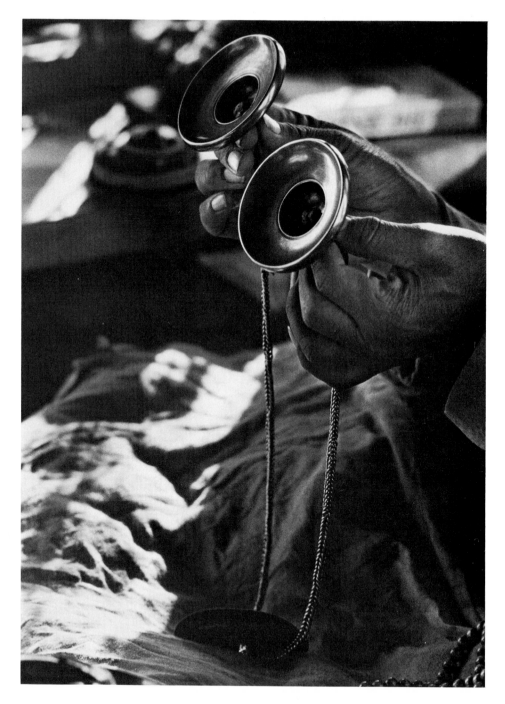

Au Leshi rings these cymbals to call the hungry ghosts. The emotion of desire plays a significant role in Buddhist psychology; it is the root of all dissatisfaction. An excess of desire manifests itself in a special realm. Like heaven, where every wish is granted, or hell, where one undergoes constant torment, there is another state of mind where nothing is enough. He calls to his hermitage these unfortunate creatures who, he explains, we cannot see, but with whom we can empathize. The typical hungry ghosts among us are those who cannot share because they think they might not have enough for themselves.

The keynote of Buddhist economics, therefore, is simplicity and non-violence. From an economist's point of view, the marvel of the Buddhist way of life is the utter rationality of its pattern — amazingly small means leading to extraordinarily satisfactory results.

For the modern economist this is very difficult to understand. He is used to measuring the "standard of living" by the amount of annual consumption, assuming all the time that a man who consumes more is "better off" than a man who consumes less. A Buddhist economist would consider this approach excessively irrational; since consumption is merely a means to human well-being, the aim should be to obtain the maximum of well-being with the minimum of consumption.

E. F. Schumacher
Small Is Beautiful

Iconographically, the hungry ghosts are represented with enormous bellies and necks like threads. Because of this anatomy, they constantly thirst. Au Leshi pours water for them to drink.

And so those, who are obsessed by stinginess, are reborn in the dark world of the Pretas and reap their reward in wretchedness.

With mouths small as the eye of a needle and bellies vast as mountains, their lot is suffering and they are tortured with the sufferings of hunger and thirst.

For reaching the limit of longing, yet kept in existence by their own deeds, they do not succeed in swallowing even the filth thrown away by others.

If man knew that such was the fruit of avarice, he would always give away even the limbs of his own body.

Aśvaghosa
The Buddhacarita: Acts of the Buddha

Au Leshi then tells the hungry ghosts that their situation, like our own, is one of illusion; any dissatisfaction they may be experiencing is nothing more than a creation of the mystery in the breast. The right hand represents the male, or suitable action, and the left, the female counterpart, or wisdom; their union points to the path out of suffering.

Wisdom-perfection is a Bodhisattva's
Mother, his father is expedient method,
For the teachers of all living beings come
Only from these two (upāya and prajñā).

. . .

Like that thing most rare, a lotus
Blossoming in a scorching fire,
He meditates amidst desires,
Which also is a thing most rare.

The Vimalakirti Nirdeśa Sūtra

Far from wishing to awaken the artist in the pupil prematurely, the teacher considers it his first task to make him a skilled artisan with sovereign control of his craft. The pupil follows out this intention with untiring industry. As though he had no higher aspirations he bows under his burden with a kind of obtuse devotion, only to discover in the course of years that forms which he perfectly masters no longer oppress but liberate. . . .

Thus the teacher lets his pupil voyage onward through himself. But the pupil, with growing receptivity, lets the teacher bring to view something of which he has often heard but whose reality is only now beginning to become tangible on the basis of his own experiences. It is immaterial what name the teacher gives it, whether indeed he names it at all. The pupil understands him even when he keeps silent.

The important thing is that an inward movement is thereby initiated. The teacher pursues it, and, without influencing its course with further instructions which would merely disturb it, helps the pupil in the most secret and intimate way he knows: by direct transference of the spirit, as it is called in Buddhist circles. "Just as one uses a burning candle to light others with," so the teacher transfers the spirit of the right art from heart to heart, that it may be illumined. If such should be granted to the pupil, he remembers that more important than all outward works, however attractive, is the inward work which he has to accomplish if he is to fulfill his vocation as an artist.

Eugen Herrigel
Zen in the Art of Archery

Au Leshi has taken a vow to teach what he knows when he is asked. He will teach anyone — man or woman, black or white, regardless of age, creed, or caste. A young Sherpa boy named Norjumbu studies the canonical proportions. After proficiency in drawing the head of the Buddha, he moves on to the body.

After completing a lesson, Norjumbu goes to the master for corrections, traditionally applied in red ink over the practice sketch.

Norjumbu, in the foreground, goes over the corrections while his uncle, Lama Yakbo, finishes breakfast. It's early in the morning, and Yakbo has just gotten out of bed. Norjumbu is his charge now that Yakbo's brother has died. They stay in a small house only five minutes from Au Leshi. Yakbo has come to learn how to die. He is old now, and he wants to be skilled in this particular art. He does not paint, save with the heart.

When Lama Yakbo is not with Au Leshi discussing impermanence, he can be found reading scriptures about impermanence in his little neighboring cottage. It is winter, and he wears a fur-lined robe.

Some early Western interpreters described Buddhism as pessimistic. Today, with more informed translations and a more complete picture of the literature and living tradition, we are able to see balance as the distinguishing characteristic of Buddhism. Every problem has a solution; every poison, an antidote; every question, an answer. In this complete, or balanced, way, Buddhists very honestly outline the realities that we all face by being alive, and a way to deal with these realities.

Now when the bardo [interval] of the moment before death dawns upon me,
I will abandon all grasping, yearning and attachment,
enter undistracted into clear awareness of the teaching,
and eject my consciousness into the space of unborn mind;
as I leave this compound body of flesh and blood
I will know it to be a transitory illusion.

The Main Verses of the Six Bardos

Contemplating the intrinsic transitoriness of our lives seems to give Yakbo insight into birth and death as some great joke. He clowns constantly, here as a profound and dour Buddha, to the guffawing delight of Norjumbu.

Laughter draws us close together in intimacy, because our egos are dissolved. The ego shell falls off in the laugh. . . . Laughter appears when the distance between the contradictory ideas is suddenly eliminated.

Katsuki Sekida
Zen Training: Methods and Philosophy

Two other students of Au Leshi, Thupten and Pasang, sometimes stay near the cave to study with him.

Thupten, a monk, was one of the first people to ask Au Leshi for instructions. He has combined painting skill with able scholarship. For a time he taught Tibetan at the Sir Edmund Hillary School in Gompa Zhung. Thupten had been married before he became a monk, and he has a small boy of eight from this marriage. In the event of divorce, Sherpa men usually take custody of the children. Now Thupten and his son Gyurmé live about an hour up the valley from Au Leshi's; they are absorbed in their respective studies—Thupten in painting and philosophy, and Gyurmé in Nepali, Tibetan, and English.

Pasang is about fifteen years younger than Thupten. His family is from Gompa Zhung, where his father is the village lama. Pasang studied for two years and divided his time between the village and Au Leshi's cave, where he worked on his drawing. Now he is married and lives in Kathmandu. The skills learned in the drawing lessons involve a way of looking at events and people as much as at deities. As a process of eliciting images from the imagination, drawing becomes a tool that can serve either the ascetic in the forest or the married city dweller.

Do not sit at home, do not go to the forest,
But recognize mind wherever you are.
When one abides in complete and perfect enlightenment,
Where is Samsara and where is Nirvana?

Saraha
Dohākosha

Au Gelung, a monk from Serlo Gompa, is another of the handful of people who have collected around Au Leshi's cave. Both a preference for living alone rather than in the monastery, and his enjoyment of Au Leshi's company, have brought him to the forest.

Not far from Au Gelung's house there is a small spring that seeps through the cracks of a large moss-encrusted boulder. Buddhist cosmology admits to certain beings known as *nagas*, or snake people, who frequently inhabit watery areas, especially springs. Their association with life-giving water and underground activity has empowered these minor deities with abilities to bestow or withhold material wealth and well-being. In addition, the snake, which sheds an old skin and emerges renewed, suggests the unveiling of interior wealth.

One day Au Gelung rather absent-mindedly washed out his dirty socks in this spring. He was subsequently smitten with a serious case of hives. Appropriate apologies and gifts to the *nagas* produced a surprisingly swift recovery.

With an enviable efficacy, belief in the *nagas* encourages a respect for both our water systems and the world of unseen but sensible forces. The *nagas* live at the source of both and retaliate if polluted. *Nagas* also appear in paintings as half-man, half-snake creatures that lend artistry and élan to hydrokinetics and psychology.

A Tibetan monk from Thupten Chöling and an old friend of Au Leshi's, Ngawong Chembi, comes to visit every now and then. Once described as Au Leshi's Tibetan radio, he enjoys recounting events in the monastery and around the valley. A teller of lusty anecdotes, he embroiders his broadcasts with a special kind of humor. Being celibate does not seem to have thwarted his ability to glean the essentials of noncelibate behavior. As a raconteur, he is not limited to the prosaic; he claims to have seen a *yeti*, or abominable snowman.

When not telling stories, Ngawong Chembi does not chatter. He can be very quiet and introspective.

As a bee without harming the flower, its colour or scent, flies away, collecting only the honey, even so should the sage wander in the village.

The Dhammapada

Diu Rimpoche, one of the many teachers with whom Au Leshi studied, also comes to visit the cave on occasion. *Diu* is the Sherpa pronunciation of the Tibetan *de phug*, which means the blissful cave, and refers to an actual spot where he spent several years in retreat. He is blind in one eye. A Tibetan, he has traveled in Nepal since the 1930s, ultimately emigrating to Nepal in the 1950s.

Diu Rimpoche is one of the few masters of a particularly difficult Tibetan text—the *Kalachakra*, or wheel of time. This work contains many astrological and medical studies. He often works with Tulshig Rimpoche to make medicines. He is not only a very highly acclaimed physician in the Tibetan tradition, but is noted for walking everywhere. Even in Kathmandu, where there are motor conveyances, he has never been known to use them.

He wears a *phurba*, or magic dagger, in his belt, hidden by his cloak. The *phurba* is magic in that he uses it to stab, or more precisely, pin down, the ego.

For the Buddhists the Vajrayāna . . . constituted a new revelation of the Buddha's doctrine, a revelation adapted to the greatly diminished possibilities of "modern man." The Kālachakratantra tells how King Sucandra went to the Buddha and asked him for the Yoga that could save the men of the kali-yuga [the current, black, or degenerate, age]. In answer, the Buddha revealed to him that the cosmos is contained in man's own body, explained the importance of sexuality, and taught him to control the temporal rhythms by disciplining respiration—thus he could escape from the domination of time. The flesh, the living cosmos, and time are the three fundamental elements of tantric sādhana [technique for realization].

Mircea Eliade
Yoga: Immortality and Freedom

E MA! [1] *a joyous and pure upland ridge,*
endowed with good fortune —
 cool summer, mild winter —
and beautified by Elysian groves . . .
but have you no friends there?

Here, there is undefiled wildlife:
the cuckoo and blackbird sing
sweet tunes in which there calls
a voice admonishing us to cast off
mundane things
 and the afflictions that are their origin;
the sweet voice of the three paths [2]
and of all spiritual continuity.

The sun's long path is a parasol on noonday's throne.
The mundane necessities, water and wood,
are richly achieved by simple efforts,
 right in manner.
The Divine Master [3] *said:*
Practice without obligation to patrons.

Within this unmade, spontaneously formed,
skull-cup shaped environment,
this is the Jālandhara of the twenty-four sacred lands,
the place of assembly of Dākas and Dākinīs. [4]

In this natural rock-nest
lives a sage, austere yogin:
he is an object of worship,
a bhiksu in manner,
with hair in long locks,
a descendant of the clan of Nyang. [5]
His small size is not disagreeable,
and though he acts as an artist,
 these icons are not for sale,
 but for spiritual accumulation.

Here, he is at ease,
 the appearances of this life abandoned:
he is content as the disciple of numerous fine masters,
 content with the unsullied vows
  of the Lesser, Greater, and Adamantine Paths,
 content with the wealth of profound learning,
 content not having obligations to others.
He has four contentments and freedom from deeds.

Regarding him, I with my many deeds,
many thoughts,
monkish form,
I gaze at the object of all my mind's aspirations —
Whatever I recall is lost in my scribbling.

When we are free from deeds,
let us undertake many deeds.

Whatever connection is made here,
I pray it be meaningful.

A LA LA! the environment and its inhabitants — how amazing!
E MA HO! in blissful good spirits,
A I A! may both goals[6] be spontaneously achieved!
A RA LI! may this give rise to auspicious splendor!

On the twenty-sixth day of the second month of the year of the Water Ox (1973), while giving to the hermitage of the Bhikṣu and Yogin Leshi the name "Pinnacle of Supreme Paradise," I, the Buddhist Bhikṣu Dharma (Tulshig Rimpoche), composed this in a sketch of recollection. May virtue increase!

Translator's Notes

1. E MA! and the various exclamations found in the final verse convey a sense of amazement and awe.

2. The three paths are those of the *śrāvaka*, the pious disciple who hangs on the words of the Buddha; the *pratyekabuddha*, the one who seeks enlightenment for himself alone; and the *bodhisattva*, the being who is dedicated to the enlightenment of all living things.

3. The Divine Master in this case is Ngawong Tenzin Norbu, the "Buddha of Dzarongpu," who was the guru of both Tulshig Rimpoche and Au Leshi.

4. Jālandhara is reckoned among the twenty-four sacred places of Ancient India. The spiritual geography of Buddhist India corresponds symbolically with the esoteric anatomy of the human body taught in the various systems of yoga.

5. Nyang is an ancient Tibetan clan from which the Lama Serwa clan of the Sherpas, to which Au Leshi belongs, is descended. Many of the notable figures in the history of the Nyingmapa school hailed from this clan.

6. The two goals of the bodhisattva are those of his own enlightenment and the enlightenment of all others.

"Have you been thinking about what I told you? Have you looked for that place from which everything comes?"

"Oh, looking real hard, huh?"

"Well, did you find it?"

RETURN

The days pass quietly with Au Leshi. One concentrates on daily activities—the lessons in painting, the preparation of meals, or the garden chores. One tries not to anticipate life or wallow in its memories. If time in the forest is spent wisely, the differences between the desirable and the repulsive diminish or disappear. Occasionally, however, the rhythm is disrupted by some event outside the small cliffside enclave; in this case, the death of a friend's father.

When a Sherpa dies, his family may call a shaman. Shamanism was practiced in Nepal and Tibet long before the introduction of Buddhism. Both the strength of the shamanic tradition and Buddhist acceptance permit men like Lhakpa Drolmi, a Buddhist, to perform rites that stem from this native religion.

The body is covered with sheets. The drum twirls slowly as the shaman begins his dance. He travels on the sound of the two-faced drum. It drones the rhythms of being, the alternating currents of life and death. He goes to the world of the dead to find the newly deceased.

The drum has a role of the first importance in shamanic ceremonies. Its symbolism is complex, its magical functions many and various. It is indispensable in conducting the shamanic séance. . . . The drumming enables the shaman to concentrate and regain contact with the spiritual world through which he is preparing to travel. . . . He can abolish time and re-establish the primordial condition of which the myths tell. . . . We are in the presence of a mystical experience that allows the shaman to transcend time and space.

Mircea Eliade
Shamanism: Archaic Techniques of Ecstasy

The drum beats faster; the shaman spins in his dance. He finds the spirit and tells him to come to this place; there are things he must be told.

Sorcerers and shamans are able, here on earth and as often as they wish, to accomplish "coming out of the body," . . . and . . . can enjoy the condition of "souls," of "disincarnate beings," which is accessible to the profane only when they die.

Mircea Eliade
Shamanism: Archaic Techniques of Ecstasy

The departed's friends and relatives fill the room. They read the parts of the scriptures, called *Bardo Thödol*, or *The Tibetan Book of the Dead*, which explain the after-death experience: "All is a creation of the mind. One should not fear what is perceived; it is as much illusion as life. One must not suffer greed or anger."

Supreme insight and illumination, and hence the greatest possibility of attaining liberation, are vouchsafed during the actual process of dying. Soon afterward, the "illusions" begin which lead eventually to reincarnation, the illuminative lights growing ever fainter and more multifarious, and the visions more and more terrifying. This descent illustrates the estrangement of consciousness from the liberating truth as it approaches nearer and nearer to physical rebirth. The purpose of the instruction is to fix the attention of the dead man, at each successive stage of delusion and entanglement, on the ever-present possibility of liberation, and to explain to him the nature of his visions. The text of the Bardo Thödol is recited by the lāma in the presence of the corpse.

. . . We are so hemmed in by things which jostle and oppress that we never get a chance, in the midst of all these "given" things, to wonder by whom they are "given." It is from this world of "given" things that the dead man liberates himself; and the purpose of the instruction is to help him towards this liberation. We, if we put ourselves in his place, shall derive no lesser reward from it, since we learn from the very first paragraphs that the "giver" of all "given" things dwells in us.

C. G. Jung
"Psychological Commentary" to The Tibetan Book of the Dead

When the service inside the house is completed, the lamas and the shaman take the body outside to a bier. Horns provide an accompaniment, and juniper smolders for incense. As the lamas file out, they distribute food used for offerings, which is now sanctified, to the mourners standing by the rail. Gompa Zhung village and Serlo Gompa can be seen in the distance.

Since outer manifestations of life have ceased, people around him may think that the person is already dead and they may wish to dispose of the corpse. But, since the inner experiences may still continue for some days, if the person is then buried or cremated it is the same as killing the person.

. . . Now the person experiences an even light similar to that which spreads across the sky before the moon rises. This happens when the white cell received from the father which during life remains at the crown cakra (psychophysical centre) descends to the heart cakra. Next the dying person experiences a dim red light such as pervades the sky at sunset. This occurs when the red cell, the fertilizing force originating from the mother, ascends from the naval cakra to the heart cakra. . . .

When these two cells meet at the heart cakra the next experience which has two stages begins. Firstly, there is complete darkness, secondly, the dying person becomes unconscious. . . .

The person now experiences empty space devoid of form or colour which, however, is not Sūnyatā [absolute emptiness]. Consciousness is now in its subtlest and will not become more refined. For ordinary people who do not know how to make use of it, this state arises and passes and is wasted. However, a person advanced in tantric practices is able to transform this most subtle state of consciousness into meditation on Sūnyatā. In this way, . . . [some] have reached Enlightenment.

Geshe Rabten
The Preliminary Practices

The food distributed, the lamas, led by the shaman, go to the bier.

Generally, after this state [of subtlest consciousness] the two cells separate and leave the body: the red cell as blood from the nose and the white cell through the urinary tract. During sleep and at death it is beneficial to lie in the lion posture in which these two signs become visible. It was thus lying on his right side that the Buddha left his human form.

The consciousness leaves the heart cakra and immediately enters the bardo body. The bardo is a very difficult phase in which the being has no freedom but is driven helplessly by the force of his own karma towards a new body, thus once more beginning the cycle of rebirth.

Geshe Rabten
The Preliminary Practices

The man on the extreme left is Tapkhay, the woodblock carver. It is his father who has died. The man with the white hat, facing the camera, is Hrita, his brother, a carpenter. Their father is in a fetal position in the bier, under an umbrella festooned with felicitous scarves.

The umbrella, which mourners secure to the bier, is a symbol of refuge that has been associated with the Buddha from earliest times. All dead people are treated as Buddhas and referred to as nobly born, regardless of the station they may have been charged with in life. Death offers a precious opportunity to break the habit of associating the self with the body, and hence to awake from delusion.

Bardo means gap; it is not only the interval of suspension after we die but also suspension in the living situation; death happens in the living situation as well. The bardo experience is part of our basic psychological make-up. There are all kinds of bardo experiences happening to us all the time, experiences of paranoia and uncertainty in everyday life; it is like not being sure of our ground, not knowing quite what we have asked for or what we are getting into. So this book is not only a message for those who are going to die and those who are already dead, but it is also a message for those who are already born; birth and death apply to everybody constantly at this very moment.

Chögyam Trungpa, Rimpoche
Commentary to *The Tibetan Book of the Dead*

The woman second from the right, holding the scarf, is the sister of the dead man's wife. When the wife died, leaving small children, this woman moved into the household and assumed her sister's responsibilities. She had had a call from a spirit of the forest many years ago and lived for two years in the woods with no clothes, listening to this being. After completing her course of study, she returned to society but was bound by a vow never to have children of her own. Her community regards her as a healer and exorcist.

Knowledge shines not in the dark, but when the darkness
Is illumined, suffering disappears (at once).
Shoots grow from the seed
And leaves from the shoots.

Saraha
Dohā kosa

A procession leaves the house and begins the ascent of a nearby mountain. They will take the dead man to the ridge, a place close to the sky. The word *sky* in many Asian languages connotes emptiness. It is fitting that this man, who has released his grasp on the flesh, is moved to that area on earth closest to space, the mountain top, where symbolically emptiness and the manifest meet.

Because the virtues of the mountain are high and broad, the power to ride the clouds is always penetrated from the mountains, and the ability to follow the wind is inevitably liberated from the mountains.

Dōgen

Shōbōgenzō-sansuikyō: The Mountains and Rivers Sutra

It is a long way to the top. At rest stops the collapsable long horns are extended, and the low drone of the death dirge piped across the cliffs and river valleys. Tapkhay is on the left, Thupten on the right. Behind them Ngawong Gendun and Ang Gelbu play smaller reed instruments.

I place before those who are the great sages lofty jewel parasols encrusted with pearls,
*   exceedingly handsome, with pleasingly shaped golden handles.*
Hereafter may delightful clouds of worship (pūjā) arise, and clouds of music and song which
*   thrill all creatures.*

*   .   .   .*

This death is not considerate of what has been done or not done; a great, sudden thunderbolt,
*   the killer as we rest, distrusted by the healthy and by the sick.*

*   .   .   .*

Whatever reality is experienced, it becomes like a thing remembered. Like a dream-experience,
*   all has gone and is not seen again.*

Sāntideva
The Bodhicaryāvatāra: Entering the Path of Enlightenment

Both the weight of the bier and the distance to the top require frequent shifts among those willing to bear the load. Here at a rest stop the shaman, with drum still twirling, goes off to relieve himself.

Death, as well as Life, is an Art, though both are often enough muddled through.

Sir John Woodroffe
Foreword to *The Tibetan Book of the Dead*

The shaman, Lhakpa Drolmi, stands framed by his traditional milieu, the forest. In his right hand he holds the drum, and in the left a trumpet made from a human thigh bone. Its sound was once described as the same as the sound you hear when you plug up your ears.

The drum announces the arrival at the top of the ridge. The cymbals chatter, and the wind whispers through the prayer flags, carrying their printed messages to anyone who listens.

The shaman goes aside to offer a special prayer. A boy holds open a text for him to read, and he blows his thigh bone trumpet. Its sound reverberates throughout the valleys, and those far below who hear the sound can imagine what is happening on the ridge above.

Rain and wind pass intermittently at 12,000 feet. A tent was erected to shelter the service to be held at the top of the ridge.

Inside the tent, lamas read the book of the dead. Spices, grains, and sanctified foodstuffs from the service that was held down below are all used as offerings.

After the service, the sack covering the body is loosened in preparation for the final rites. Tapkhay holds his father's head.

Thus shall [you] think of all this fleeting world:
A star at dawn, a bubble in a stream;
A flash of lightning in a summer cloud,
A flickering lamp, a phantom, and a dream.

The Diamond Sutra: Vajrachchedikaprajñāpāramitā Sutra

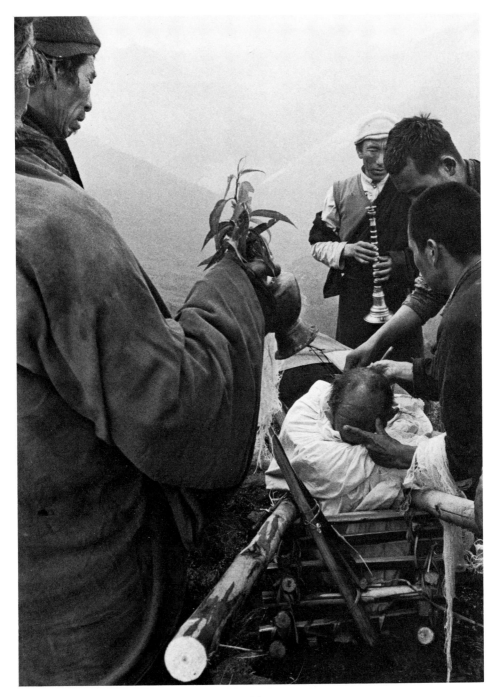

The shaman stands over the body holding a *pumba*, a sacrificial pot containing water that, when sanctified, becomes nectar. The man in black holds a woodblock print of a *maṇḍala*, folded into a square, then wrapped with five colored threads.

This *maṇḍala* is like a map for the deceased. The thread wrapping and the images of the Buddhas of the five directions printed on the paper inside remind the dead person that he must be alert lest negligence, greed, anger, arrogance or jealousy arise and obscure his newly found clarity with fantasy.

The head is anointed with consecrated water.

When you do not realize that you are one with the river, or with the universe, you have fear. Whether it is separated into drops or not, water is water. Our life and death are the same thing. When we realize this fact we have no fear of death anymore, and we have no actual difficulty in our life. . . . For us, just now, we have some fear of death, but after we resume our true original nature, there is Nirvana. That is why we say, "To attain Nirvana is to pass away." "To pass away" is not a very adequate expression. Perhaps "to pass on," or "to go on," or "to join" would be better. Will you try to find some better expression for death? When you find it, you will have quite a new interpretation of your life.

Shunryu Suzuki
Zen Mind, Beginner's Mind

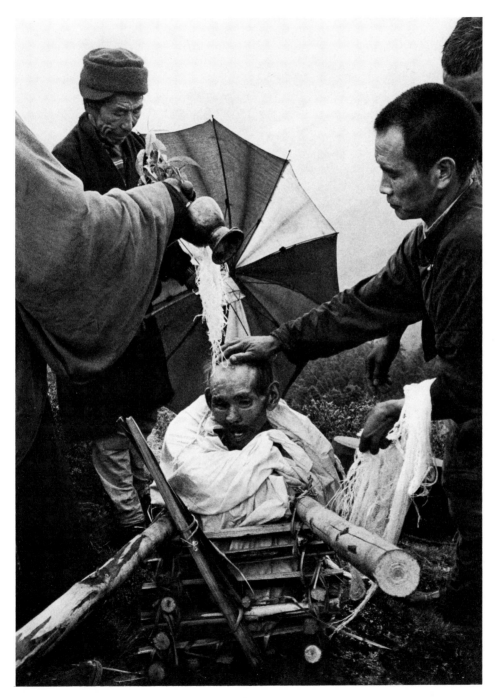

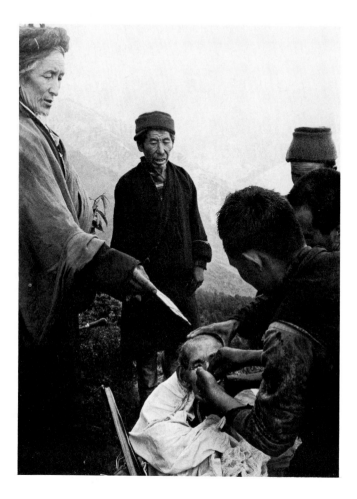

As the shaman touches the paper print to the head, the other men knead butter in their hands.

They place these firm butter wads in the eye sockets and the mouth. A symbol of life and nourishment, the butter recalls the cyclical aspect of death, an end in only one sense, but more importantly, a movement in a continuum.

Those mourners fit and able were requested to gather wood for the pyre from a nearby forest. They brought back logs and stacked them between two old stone cairns. As the body is lifted to the top of the pyre, the mourners circumambulate these two cairns. In the foreground, Hrita, the dead man's lay son, stands stunned from the events of the day.

Tapkhay, the deceased's cleric son, makes a final adjustment to the bier surmounting the pyre. Throughout these proceedings, Tapkhay was able to exercise his training as a lama and direct the course of his father's passage. When I asked him whether it would be appropriate to make a photographic record of the funeral, he responded with enthusiasm, saying that this way people would know he had done right by his father.

As the fire crackles and smolders in the thin air, a neighboring mourner points out that it is very auspicious to warm oneself by such a blaze.

Though everyone lives seeking personal enjoyment,
This body at some time
Will be reduced to a mere handful of ash.
Ask: "Oh, Master of the body!
What is the 'True-I'?"

Meditation Master Ku San Sunim
Nine Mountains

As the last remaining attachment to this life rises in smoke, the deceased continues to the great initiation awaiting us all. The clouds break slightly and reveal Ulla Tashi Palchen, one of the Himalayan peaks that loom over the valley where he spent a life. The village of Gompa Zhung sits by the riverside; up to the left, the little white speck of Serlo monastery, where his son learned the intricacies of his culture and how to direct his father at this concurrence of planes.

Like salt sea water that turns
Sweet when drunk up by the clouds,
So a firm mind that works for others turns
The poison of sense-objects into nectar.

Saraha
Dohākoṣa

REFERENCES

These references give bibliographic information for the extracts used in the text; they are not intended to provide a general guide to the literature on the subjects discussed in this book. The page numbers at the end of each citation correlate a quotation with its appearance in the source; for example, "p. 204 (*RHV*, 164)" indicates that the extract on page 164 of *Rhythms of a Himalayan Village* is taken from page 204 of the source.

Aśvaghoṣa. *The Buddhacarita: Acts of the Buddha.* Translated by E. H. Johnston. Lahore, Pakistan: University of the Panjab, published for the University by the Baptist Mission Press, Calcutta, 1935–36. Reprint ed. (2 vols. in 1), Delhi: Motilal Banarsidass, 1972; *iv*, 59, 60, p. 53 (*RHV*, 17); *xiv*, 29–30, p. 206 (*RHV*, 148).

Aziz, B. N. "Views from the Monastery Kitchen." *Kailash* (Kathmandu) 4, no. 2 (1976): 155–167; p. 165 (*RHV*, 30); p. 160 (*RHV*, 31).

Bṛihad-Āraṇyaka Upanishad. In *The Thirteen Principal Upanishads,* translated by Robert Ernest Hume. 2nd ed., London: Oxford University Press, 1931. Oxford University Paperback, 1971; 1.5.3, p. 87 (*RHV*, 128).

Conze, Edward; Horner, I. B.; Snellgrove, D.; Waley, A., eds. *Buddhist Texts Through the Ages.* Oxford: Bruno Cassirer, 1954. Torchbook ed., New York: Harper & Row, 1964; p. 238 (*RHV*, 161); p. 296 (*RHV*, 132).

Coomaraswamy, Ananda K. "Chinese Painting at Boston." In *Coomaraswamy,* edited by Roger Lipsey. 3 vols., vol. 1. Princeton: Princeton University Press, 1977; Bollingen Series LXXXIX; p. 308 (*RHV*, 9).

————. *Domestic Handicraft and Culture* (pp. 8 ff., 14–15 [1910]). Quoted in *Coomaraswamy,* vol. 3; pp. 52–53 (*RHV*, 87).

————. "A Lecture on Comparative Religion [1944, unpublished]." Quoted in *Coomaraswamy,* vol. 3; p. 276 (*RHV*, 139).

————. *The Transformation of Nature in Art.* Cambridge: Harvard University Press, 1934. Reprint ed., New York: Dover, 1956; pp. 5–6 (*RHV*, 130); pp. 17–18 (*RHV*, 109).

Dasgupta, Shashi Bhushan. *An Introduction to Tantric Buddhism.* Calcutta: Calcutta University Press, 1958. Reprint ed., Berkeley: Shambhala, 1974; p. 65 (*RHV*, 63).

Dasgupta, Surama. *Development of Moral Philosophy in India.* Calcutta: Orient Longmans, 1961; p. 175 (*RHV*, 69).

The Dhammapada. Translated by Nārada Thera. Colombo (Sri Lanka): Vajirārāma, 1972; verse 201 (XV, 5), p. 175 (*RHV*, 46); verses 58-59 (IV, 15–16), pp. 59–60 (*RHV*, 51) — the first paragraph of this extract explains the verses, the second is a translator's footnote to the verses; verse 49 (IV, 6), p. 53 (*RHV*, 164).

The Diamond Sutra: Vajrachchedikaprajñāpāramitā Sutra. Translated by A. F. Price. In *The Diamond Sutra and the Sutra of Hui Neng,* translated by A.F. Price and Wong Mou-Lam. Berkeley: Shambhala, 1969; p. 74 (*RHV*, 210). The lines quoted were originally translated by Kenneth Saunders in *Lotuses of the Mahayana,* edited by Kenneth Saunders. London: John Murray, 1924, p. 11.

Dīgha-nikāya. Translated by Bhikkhu Nāṇamoli. In *The Life of the Buddha,* translated and edited by Bhikkhu Nāṇamoli.

Kandy (Sri Lanka): Buddhist Publication
Society, 1972; *D.* 16, p. 335 (*RHV*, 70).

Dōgen. *Shōbōgenzō-sansuikyō: The Mountains and
Rivers Sutra.* Translated by Carl W. Biele-
feldt. In *The Mountain Spirit*, edited by
Michael Charles Tobias and Harold
Drasdo. Woodstock, N.Y.: Overlook Press,
1979; p. 41 (*RHV*, 197).

Dutt, Sukumar. *Buddhist Monks and Monasteries
of India.* London: George Allen & Unwin,
1962; p. 161 (*RHV*, 24).

Eliade, Mircea. *The Myth of the Eternal Return:
Cosmos and History.* Translated by Willard
R. Trask. Princeton: Princeton University
Press, 1954; Princeton/Bollingen Paper-
back, 1971; Bollingen Series XLVI; p. 95
(*RHV*, 32).

―――. *The Sacred and the Profane: The Nature of
Religion.* Translated by Willard R. Trask.
New York: Harcourt, Brace & World,
1959; A Harvest Book, n.d.; p. 14 (*RHV*, 94).

―――. *Shamanism: Archaic Techniques of Ecstasy.*
Translated by Willard R. Trask. Princeton:
Princeton University Press, 1964; Prince-
ton/Bollingen Paperback, 1972; Bollingen
Series LVI; pp. 168, 171 (*RHV*, 180);
p. 479 (*RHV*, 182).

―――. *Yoga: Immortality and Freedom.* Translated by Willard R. Trask. Princeton:
Princeton University Press, 1969; Prince-
ton/Bollingen Paperback, 1970; Bollingen
Series LVI; p. 204 (*RHV*, 166).

Evans-Wentz, W. Y., ed. *The Tibetan Book of
the Dead.* Foreword by Sir John Woodroffe,
Psychological Commentary by C. G. Jung.
3rd ed., New York: Oxford University
Press, 1957; Oxford University Press,
Galaxy Books, 1960; pp. *xxxvi, xxxix-xl*
(*RHV*, 185); *lxvii* (*RHV*, 201).

―――, ed. *The Tibetan Book of the Great Liberation.* London: Oxford University Press,
1954; Oxford University Press Paperback,
1968; pp. 25–26 (*RHV*, 140).

―――, ed. *Tibetan Yoga and Secret Doctrines.*
2nd ed., London: Oxford University Press,

1958; Oxford University Press Paperback,
1967; p. 65 (*RHV*, 144).

―――, ed. *Tibet's Great Yogi Milarepa.* 2nd ed.,
London: Oxford University Press Paperback, 1969; p. 31 (*RHV*, 120).

Fremantle, Francesca, and Trungpa, Chögyam,
trans. *The Tibetan Book of the Dead.* Commentary
by Chögyam Trungpa. Boulder: Shambhala,
1975; pp. 1–2 (*RHV*, 193); pp. 98–99
(*RHV*, 156).

Guenther, Herbert V., trans. *The Royal Song
of Saraha: A Study in the History of Buddhist
Thought.* Seattle: University of Washington
Press, 1968; Berkeley: Shambhala, 1973;
p. 65 (*RHV*, 222); p. 66 (*RHV*, 2); p. 67
(*RHV*, 194).

Herrigel, Eugen. *Zen in the Art of Archery.*
Translated by R. F. C. Hull. New York:
Pantheon Books, 1953; New York: Random
House, Vintage Books, 1971; pp. 63,
67–68 (*RHV*, 152).

Jung, C. G. "Psychological Commentary."
Translated by R. F. C. Hull. In *The Tibetan
Book of the Dead*, edited by W. Y. Evans-
Wentz; pp. *xxxvi, xxxix-xl* (*RHV*, 185).

Ku San Sunim. *Nine Mountains.* Chogye
Chonglim (Republic of Korea): Song Kwang
Sa Monastery, 1977; p. 75 (*RHV*, 221).

The Main Verses of the Six Bardos. In *The
Tibetan Book of the Dead*, translated by
F. Fremantle and C. Trungpa; pp. 98–99
(*RHV*, 156).

Milarepa. *The Hundred Thousand Songs of Milarepa.*
Translated by Garma C. C. Chang. 2 vols.,
vol. 1. New Hyde Park, N.Y.: University
Books, 1962; Boulder: Shambhala, 1977;
pp. 190–191 (*RHV*, 5); p. 204 (*RHV*, 113).

Milindapañha: Questions of Milinda. In *World of
the Buddha*, edited by Lucien Stryk. Garden
City, N.Y.: Doubleday, 1968; Anchor
Books, 1969; pp. 94–96 (*RHV*, 99).

Ñāṇamoli Bhikkhu. Preface to *The Path
of Purification: Visuddhi Magga*, by Buddha-
ghosa, translated by Bhikkhu Ñāṇamoli.
3rd ed., Kandy (Sri Lanka): Buddhist

Publication Society, 1975; pp. *vii–viii* (*RHV*, 27); p. *xxxi* (*RHV*, 123).

Nebesky-Wojkowitz, René de. *Oracles and Demons of Tibet*. s'Gravenhage: Mouton, 1956; Graz, Austria: Akademische Druck- und Verlaganstalt, 1975; pp. 347, 353 (*RHV*, 43).

Ocean of Delight for the Wise. Translated by Lāma Kazi Dawa-Samdup. In *Tibetan Yoga*, edited by W. Y. Evans-Wentz; verse 188, p. 65 (*RHV*, 144).

Olson, Eleanor. "The Meditations and the Rituals." In *The Art of Tibet*, by Pratapaditya Pal. New York: Asia Society, 1969; p. 46 (*RHV*, 65).

The Platform Scripture. Translated by Wing-Tsit Chan. New York: St. John's University Press, 1963 (Asian Institute Translations, no. 3); pp. 91–93 (*RHV*, 137).

Pott, Peter H. "Tibet." In *The Art of Burma, Korea, Tibet*, by A. B. Griswold, Chewon Kim, and Pott. New York: Crown Publishers, 1964; p. 176 (*RHV*, 111); pp. 181–82 (*RHV*, 35).

Prajñāpāramitā-Ratnaguṇasaṃcayagāthā: Verses on the Perfection of Wisdom. In *The Perfection of Wisdom in Eight Thousand Lines and Its Verse Summary*, translated by Edward Conze. Bolinas, Cal.: Four Seasons Foundation, 1973 (Wheel Series 1); verses 44–45, (II, 9–10), p. 14 (*RHV*, 125).

Geshe Rabten. *The Preliminary Practices*. Translated by Venerable Gonsar Tulku. Dharamsala (H.P.), India: Library of Tibetan Works and Archives, 1974; pp. 13–14 (*RHV*, 186); p. 14 (*RHV*, 188).

Rechung. *Jetsün-Kahbum: Biography of Milarepa*. Translated by Lāma Kazi Dawa-Samdup. In *Tibet's Great Yogī: Milarepa*, edited by W. Y. Evans-Wentz; p. 31 (*RHV*, 120).

Rin-chen gter-mdzod. Translated by David Snellgrove. In *Himalayan Pilgrimage*, by David Snellgrove. Oxford: Bruno Cassirer, 1961; p. 145 (*RHV*, 60).

Śāntideva. *Entering the Path of Enlightenment: Bodhicaryāvatāra*. Translated by Marion L. Matics. New York: Macmillan, 1970; II, 19, 20, 34, 37, pp. 149–150 (*RHV*, 198); V, 60–64, pp. 167–168 (*RHV*, 142).

Saraha. *Dohākosa*. Translated by David Snellgrove. In *Buddhist Texts*, edited by Edward Conze et al.; verse 103, p. 238 (*RHV*, 161). Translated by Herbert V. Guenther. In *Royal Song*; verse 11, p. 65 (*RHV*, 222); verse 17, p. 66 (*RHV*, 2); verse 19, p. 67 (*RHV*, 194).

Saunders, E. Dale. *Mudrā*. New York: Pantheon Books, 1960; Bollingen Series LVIII; pp. 146–47 (*RHV*, 72); p. 150 (*RHV*, 38).

Schumacher, E. F. *Small Is Beautiful*. London: Blond & Briggs, 1973; New York: Harper & Row, 1973; p. 54 (*RHV*, 147).

Sekida, Katsuki. *Zen Training: Methods and Philosophy*. New York: John Weatherhill, 1975; p. 151 (*RHV*, 158).

Seng-ts'an. *On Truth in the Heart*. Translated by Arthur Waley. In *Buddhist Texts*, edited by Edward Conze et al.; p. 296 (*RHV*, 132).

Stcherbatsky, T. [Fyodor Ippolitovich]. *Buddhist Logic*. 2 vols., vol. 1. Leningrad: Academy of Sciences of the USSR, 1930–1932 (Bibliotheca Buddhica XXVI); New York: Dover, 1962; p. 2 (*RHV*, 83).

Stein, R. A. *Tibetan Civilization*. Translated by J. E. Stapleton Driver. London: Faber and Faber, 1972; Stanford, Cal.: Stanford University Press, 1972; pp. 281–82 (*RHV*, 107).

Suzuki, Daisetz T. *Outlines of Mahayana Buddhism*. London: Luzac & Co., 1907; New York: Schocken Books, 1963; p. 36 (*RHV*, 18).

Suzuki, Shunryu. *Zen Mind, Beginner's Mind*. New York: John Weatherhill, 1970; p. 90 (*RHV*, 214).

Thogs-med bzang-po. *rGyal-sgrag lag-len so-bdun-ma (Thirty-Seven Practices of All Buddhas' Sons)*. In *The Thirty-Seven Practices of All Buddhas' Sons and The Prayer of the Virtuous, Beginning, Middle, and End*, by Thogs-med bzang-po and rJe Tzong-kha-pa, translated by Geshe Ngawong Dhargyey, Sherpa Tulku, Khamlung Tulku, Alexander Berzin, and Jonathan Landaw. Rev. ed., Dharamsala (H.P.), India: Library of Tibetan Works and Archives, 1975; verses 20–21, pp. 10–11 (*RHV*, 135).

Trungpa, Chögyam, Rimpoche. Commentary on *The Tibetan Book of the Dead*. In *The Tibetan Book of the Dead*, translated by F. Fremantle and C. Trungpa; pp. 1–2 (*RHV*, 193).

Tulshig Rimpoche. Poems on pages 21 and 169–70 (*RHV*) were composed by Tulshig Dharmamati (Tulshig Rimpoche) and translated from the Tibetan by Matthew Kapstein.

The Vimalakīrti Nirdeśa Sūtra. Translated by Charles Luk [Lu K'uan Yu]. Berkeley: Shambhala, 1972; p. 90 (*RHV*, 150).

Woodroffe, Sir John. Foreword to *The Tibetan Book of the Dead*. In *The Tibetan Book of the Dead*, edited by W. Y. Evans-Wentz; p. *lxvii* (*RHV*, 201).